Foreword

I was probably a teenager when I heard an old saying that, even in my youth I thought to be quite profound: "A ship is safe in the harbor; but that's not what ships are built for." I've thought about that quotation many times over the years, and it helps me when I've been tempted to choose inaction instead of action, safety instead of risk, and complacency instead of courage.

Today, as an adult, I've seen enough of life to convince me that the old saying needs to be re-posted, re-tweeted and re-released....in technicolor! My children are growing up in a world that often seeks to minimize any discomfort, any problems, any challenges, as if these types of situations have no business happening or were never supposed to be part of life. What kind of life would that be? Just a bunch of ships that stay in the harbor and never venture out to sea? No adventure? No growth? No progress? No way!

Anxiety, fear, and nervousness *are* a part of life, and while it is certain that people experience them in different and sometimes extreme degrees, they can be better managed and understood and perhaps, with practice and patience, replaced with a measure of faith and hope.

In this book, Dr. Morgan will talk to you like a friend. You won't feel like you're being preached to, but like you're listening to a really good Gospel Doctrine instructor who has found insights regarding anxiety in the scriptures that you've never even noticed before.

David Morgan is professionally trained, but if he hadn't put "PhD" it on the cover you wouldn't know it. He shares many personal and family experiences with anxiety that will make you less, well, *anxious* as you read. You will learn scripture-based strategies and principles that will make a real difference in your life, whether you or a loved one is dealing with anxiety. I am grateful for this resource which I expect to refer to again and again. Time to set sail. Bon voyage!

-John Bytheway

Peace Be Unto You

David T. Morgan, PhD

Published by David T. Morgan, PhD Inc
Vancouver, Washington

Acknowledgments

I never thought that writing an anxiety book would make me anxious. Perhaps it has been for the best; it's always easier to help others with their troubles when you've had personal experience with the same. I am truly grateful to so many people who have helped me along the way and made this experience less stressful. My parents, brothers and sisters have been continually supportive and a great source of strength. I love them very much. I'm thankful to my good friends who provided reviews of earlier manuscripts, including Jeff Madsen and Marilyn Harker. Others were extremely helpful in finding typos and other mistakes. I'm forever grateful to the eagle eyes and attentive minds of Janae Smith, Deena Morgan, Janet Peterson and Sharyle Karren. I'm very thankful to have made the acquaintance of John Bytheway and for his helpful suggestions, including his very generous offer to write the foreword. I cannot say enough about my amazing editor, Bonnie Brien. Her excellent knowledge of writing is matched by her wonderful understanding of the gospel of Jesus Christ. She has been a tremendous and indispensable help.

I'm so thankful for my children who have been a source of joy for as long as I've been a father. I'm very proud of the people they are becoming. Finally, none of this would have ever happened if it weren't for the ongoing support and loving kindness of my remarkable wife, Kristyn. She is my inspiration, my rock, my role model, and my eternal sweetheart. I'm forever grateful for her patience and tolerance of my shortcomings. I owe everything I have to her.

Introduction

When I was an adolescent, I wanted to become a child psychiatrist. I'm not exactly sure why, but the idea of a career in the mental health field appealed to me. Becoming a psychiatrist would involve the completion of medical school after premedical undergraduate work. I attended my freshman year at BYU and took general classes, including psychology. After returning from my mission two years later, I got serious about premedical training. Yet I was concerned about my ability to succeed with this. I'd had a previous experience where I witnessed a minor medical procedure and almost passed out. I remember thinking, "I'm not sure I'm cut out for medicine if I can't even *watch* someone getting stitches." After that, I enrolled in an extremely competitive biology class. It was completely overwhelming. I dropped the class and started to look at other options in mental health. Psychology was a clear choice, and I completed bachelor's and master's degrees.

While in the master's program, I thought seriously about eventually becoming a professor and teaching at BYU. I had great admiration for the faculty in the program and believe they heavily influenced my thoughts about a future career. My professors counseled that if I wanted to eventually teach at BYU, I should get a doctorate somewhere other than BYU to increase my chances of being hired, as BYU did not typically hire applicants who received all of their training at one institution. As the time for doctoral program applications approached, I considered many different possibilities. I eventually applied to thirteen different doctoral programs, getting accepted to only two: BYU and the University of North Dakota. I was not enticed by the frequent subzero temperatures and remote location of North Dakota, having grown up in sunny California. BYU winters were plenty cold for me, and therefore I felt I was left with a single choice. I would pursue my doctorate at Brigham Young University. I lamented the fact that this would significantly decrease my chances to ever teach at BYU. However, I had no idea what great blessings this would eventually bring.

My doctoral training required a one-year, full-time internship. I chose to wait until the last year of my program to do this, meaning I would graduate upon completion of the internship. Similar to applying for doctoral programs, this process involved applications and then waiting to hear about acceptance. Eager to not repeat my experience of being accepted to only two doctoral programs, I applied to almost twenty internships, trying to increase chances of success. The notification process for internships was different from doctoral program admissions. Instead of getting acceptance or rejection letters, all of the internship notifications happened on the same day. Several months after applying, potential interns would wait by the phone on a predetermined date. During a specific four-hour period on that day, all internships would call and inform applicants of acceptance. If your phone didn't ring, that meant you were not selected for an internship and would have to wait until the following year. That would also mean a *full year* delay in completing my education, which was basically unacceptable to me. My anxiety built as that day approached. *What if no one selected me?* I had already finished my doctoral coursework. My dissertation was in full swing and would be completed within a year. A one-year delay due to a missed internship was definitely not part of the plan. Again, there was nothing I could do at that point except pray and hope. There was much prayer, but I will admit my anxiety created some barriers to hope.

The day arrived, and I sat in our den in a cold sweat. This was back in the days prior to cell phones, so I sat alone in the room, staring at the phone. It rang a couple of times, but the calls were unrelated to internship issues. I remember trying to finish those calls as soon as possible, having a sense of panic that if an internship called and they got a busy signal, they might not call back. Three of the four hours passed without a single internship call. My mind raced. I anticipated worst-case scenarios. I was filled with self-doubt. It was a terrible few hours. Finally, the phone rang. It was an internship in Portland, Oregon. They offered me an interview and I readily accepted. It was the only internship offer I received, and I was profoundly grateful. Some weeks later I went to the interview. I discovered that the internship setting was a community counseling center, and among other things they did a fair amount of work in psychological evaluation. I had some experience in psychological evaluation, so that eased my fears to a certain extent. However, I also discovered that an intern in the previous year had been terminated from the internship due to underwhelming performance in conducting psychological evaluations. That increased my anxiety. My only option for internship apparently had a record of terminating interns. They offered me the internship and I accepted, as the only other choice was to wait a year. I determined I would do the best I could, relying on a small bit of confidence that I had some prior evaluation experience to build upon.

Six months later, we moved from Provo, Utah to the greater Portland area so I could begin the internship. On the first day, we received more information regarding the requirement to complete psychological evaluations. We were also informed that our first psychological evaluation would be scheduled for the following week, where we would meet with a client and begin test administration. It became clear that we were expected to know how to administer and interpret over two dozen different psychological tests. Some of them I had been trained on, some of them I had no training but had heard of them, and others I had never even heard of. The internship supervisors simply assumed we knew how to do these tests, and I wasn't about to acknowledge my lack of mastery in these areas. I had been trained in the administration of many different psychological tests and was familiar with the general process. I borrowed the administration manuals to the tests I was unfamiliar with and studied them over the weekend. Most of them were simple and easy to learn. However, there was one that was on the required list that sent my anxiety through the roof. It was the Rorschach Inkblot Test. This test hails from old psychodynamic theory and was not used very often. However, it was on the list. As I researched the training for this instrument, I found that universities that did such training often took *two full semesters* to provide such education. I had one weekend to learn it. I straight-up panicked. While I could probably bluff my way through some of the other required tests and learn as I go, there was no way I could fake it on the Rorschach. My lack of ability would be made manifest in clear detail, with no recourse. One of the interns from the year prior had been terminated due to lack of skill in psychological evaluation. I feared I was headed for the same outcome. What happened if you got terminated from an internship? I didn't even know, but I worried I had doomed my career, my ability to support my family, and the rest of my life in general.

Thankfully, one of the faculty members at the internship was designated as our mentor. I confided my dilemma in him. He was very supportive and challenged my catastrophic thinking. He reasoned there was no cause for me to worry, as I had never had the chance to learn the Rorschach. If the internship team wanted me to administer such a test, and was willing to teach it to me, then I would be willing to learn. While his logic was inscrutable, my anxiety remained. I envisioned being belittled by my supervisors or chastised for having shown up to a predoctoral internship so poorly prepared. Nevertheless, the way forward was clear. Our first evaluation seminar was on the last day of the first week of training. I had to talk with the supervisor who was over psychological evaluations and explain to him that I was unprepared to administer the Rorschach. I planned my interaction carefully. If he was going to berate me, I didn't want him to have a lot of time to do it. So, I decided that I would talk to him right after the seminar ended, as he was leaving to go home for the weekend. I even thought it would be good to approach him as he was waiting for the elevator to go to his car. I mean, he probably wouldn't miss his chance to take the elevator just to chew me out, right? I can clearly remember that moment, as my courage barely eclipsed my terror.

"Dr. Benson, can I talk with you for just a minute?" I said as he pressed the elevator call button.

"Sure, David; what's on your mind?"

I took a large breath. "I just wanted to let you know that I don't know how to administer the Rorschach. They never taught us how to do it in my coursework so I'm really sorry but if someone is willing to teach me then I'm willing to learn." I exhaled loudly.

"Oh, I wouldn't worry about it. It's an outdated test that I don't like to use much anyway, so I'm not requiring it. Have a great weekend." Dr. Benson later confirmed his preferred testing instrument was one where I had considerable experience, and my skill of interpretation on that test practically rivaled his.

I think one of the only good things about anxiety is the incomparable feeling of relief that comes after the anxiety is gone. I left the internship site that afternoon feeling ten times lighter than I had in previous days. The rest of my internship proceeded without major incident. There were moments of trial and good learning experiences, but all eventually went as I had hoped. Now, more than twenty years later, I see the absolute wisdom in the way things worked out. I never did go to teach at BYU but have instead worked as a psychologist in private practice. Getting all of my education at BYU has been one of the richest blessings in my life. It has enabled me to view psychology through a gospel lens, therefore being able to weed out the false and embrace the true. Living in the Pacific Northwest has been a tremendous opportunity for our family. Our children have wonderful friends in an area where the Church is relatively small but very strong.

As my experience suggests, anxiety does not exist in and of itself, and this is one of the things you will learn by reading this book. I understand there are times when anxiety feels as if it has its own motor and is completely in control, but that is not accurate. Perceptions fuel anxiety. Perceptions can become very automatic and happen outside of our consciousness, which is one of the reasons anxiety often feels out of control. However, the way we perceive things determines how we feel about them. If we can change the way we think, we will absolutely change the way we feel.

My intention with this book is to provide practical strategies to manage anxiety, using a combination of psychological principles and gospel truths. As I have worked with people throughout the years who seek relief from anxiety, they almost always say the same thing. They want something practical. They want strategies they can use in their everyday lives. I have done my best to provide such strategies. However, there is something that goes beyond practical strategies, which I consider more important. As you read this book, I want you to develop a feeling of hope. There are so many who have dealt with anxiety for so long, they have lost hope. I want people to understand change is always possible, even when very difficult. As you read, I truly wish you will be filled with a greater sense of empowerment, motivation, and lasting hope that you can gain relief from some of the challenges that come from anxiety.

CHAPTER ONE

Anxiety Is A Part of Life

"For it must needs be, that there is an opposition in all things. If not so, my firstborn in the wilderness, righteousness could not be brought to pass, neither wickedness, neither holiness nor misery, neither good nor bad. Wherefore, all things must needs be a compound in one; wherefore, if it should be one body it must needs remain as dead, having no life neither death, nor corruption nor incorruption, happiness nor misery, neither sense nor insensibility." (2 Nephi 2:11)

"For it must needs be, that there is an opposition in all things. If not so, my firstborn in the wilderness, righteousness could not be brought to pass, neither wickedness, neither holiness nor misery, neither good nor bad. Wherefore, all things must needs be a compound in one; wherefore, if it should be one body it must needs remain as dead, having no life neither death, nor corruption nor incorruption, happiness nor misery, neither sense nor insensibility." (2 Nephi 2:11)

I remember once talking with a woman who told me she had anxiety issues. When I asked her to describe her experience, she said, "Have you ever been out for a walk, minding your own business, and then out of nowhere a dog rushes out and starts barking at you?" I told her I had been in such situations, even just a few days prior. She replied, "What did you feel like?" I remarked how I was very startled. My heart rate jumped, breathing grew shallow, and I felt great fear. It was an automatic and immediate response, requiring no thought on my part. I told her it was an uncomfortable feeling as well. She sighed and said, "I feel like that all the time."

"I feel like that all the time." Such is the case for many who experience chronic anxiety. Anxiety is designed to be helpful, increasing

our awareness and physical capacities for small moments. Some have described this as a "fight or flight" response. Yet these moments are intended to be short and in reaction to true threats. Those who have anxiety disorders have such feelings on a very regular basis, and often in response to threats that are not truly dangerous, but only seem so.

For example, when one of our sons was twelve years old, he was asked to give a short talk to our ward of about 100 people. He accepted the assignment but was very nervous about it. His anxiety increased over time, and he ultimately wanted to back out at the last minute. I remember the morning he was supposed to give the talk. We had not yet left home to go to church. He was in a full-blown panic, hyperventilating and in great distress. His body was reacting as if he were in physical danger, the same as if he were being chased by a bear or dangled from the edge of a cliff. My remarkable wife sat him down and explained to him that 1) there was no actual danger, even though his mind felt otherwise, and 2) the long-term solution to this anxiety was to press forward and confront the fear. Our son agreed to give the talk. It was a very anxious experience for him, but he completed the task.

One might ask, "Why would you require him to do something that caused such distress? Wouldn't a loving parent intervene and stop the anxious situation from happening?" The answer to this question lies in an understanding of the long-term benefits of difficult tasks. The story of our first parents and their initial experiences on earth is instructive. The Garden of Eden was prepared by God, beautifully designed with vegetation, including fruit-bearing trees and other plants. When Adam and Eve were placed in the garden, they were advised they could partake of any of the available fruit, with one exception. "And the Lord God commanded the man, saying, Of every tree of the garden thou mayest freely eat: But of the tree of the knowledge of good and evil, thou shalt not eat of it: for in the day that thou eatest thereof thou shalt surely die" (Genesis 2:16-17). To the best of our knowledge, there was no barbed wire fence surrounding the tree of knowledge of good and evil. There was no large sign with skull and crossbones stating, "DO NOT EAT; IF YOU DO YOU WILL DIE." It appears Father in Heaven created this tree and fruit within full view and access of His children, the effect of partaking thereof being *death*, and simply gave a verbal warning about the consequences. This begs the question, why wouldn't He have done more to prevent access to such a dangerous fruit? Why not put that fruit far out of reach of His children? *Why even plant the tree in the first place?*

Lehi explains this situation as he counsels with his son Jacob: "And to bring about *his eternal purposes in the end of man*, after he had created our first parents, and the beasts of the field and the fowls of the air, and in fine, all things which are created, it must needs be that there was an opposition; even the forbidden fruit in opposition to the tree of life; the one being sweet and the other bitter. Wherefore, the Lord God gave unto man that he should act for himself. Wherefore, man could not act for himself save it should be that he was enticed by the one or the other" (2 Nephi 2:15-16, emphasis added). What does Lehi mean by "his eternal purposes in the end of man?" This is another way of saying "God's long-term designs for his children" or "what Father in Heaven wants for his children in the eternal perspective." So, what are God's long-term goals for His children?

The scriptures give greater understanding to God's purposes for us. "For behold, this is my work and my glory—to bring to pass the immortality and eternal life of man" (Moses 1:39). This two-fold purpose indicates our Father in Heaven wants us to overcome the effects of physical death (immortality) and to live like He does (eternal life). One of the primary effects of the Atonement of Jesus Christ is the gift of resurrection. Because of the Fall of Adam, all born in mortality will die, but thanks to Jesus Christ, that same group will be raised from the dead to never die again (see 1 Corinthians 15:22 and Alma 11:42-43). Thus, God's first declared purpose of "bringing to pass immortality" has been fulfilled. The second purpose, eternal life, is different from immortality. Eternal life is to live with God, live like He lives, and is the "greatest of all the gifts of God" (D&C 14:7). Unlike resurrection, the gift of eternal life comes only as we are obedient to the commandments and faithful to our covenants.

We also know that this world was created so we can have the experiences that will help us become like our Father in Heaven. Referring to the creation, God stated, "We will go down, for there is space there, and we will take of these materials, and we will make an earth whereon these may dwell; *And we will prove them herewith, to see if they will do all things whatsoever the Lord their God shall command them*" (Abraham 3:24-25, emphasis added). Hence, a primary purpose of this life is to be tried and proven, to see if we will do those things that we have been commanded to do. Just like any good test would be a rigorous examination of a person's knowledge and abilities in a certain discipline, the "test of life" is a rigorous examination of our determination to choose the right under difficult circumstances. Let's review the principles previously outlined:

- God has created opposition in the world, and we are tempted to choose one way or another
- One of the primary reasons for this opposition is to bring to pass God's goals for His children
- Achieving eternal life is one of God's main intentions for the human race
- Eternal life can only be attained as we are tested and tried through difficulty

Perhaps this gives greater perspective regarding why life can be difficult at times, and why we are required to pass through trials. Sometimes we view trials as curses, or a deviation from the heavenly plan. However, I believe trials are *exactly* what we need in order to grow and become like our Father in Heaven. Recently my wife was telling me about a friend who has a son on a mission. Her friend made a comment along these lines: "Before our son went on a mission, we had heard about all the great blessings that come to families when their children are missionaries. We looked forward to that. However, since he has been on a mission, we have had an increase in trials in our lives. I'm not sure why we aren't being blessed like other families with missionary children." My heart went out to this good sister, and at the same time I thought, "What makes you think those so-called trials are not actually blessings?"

Suppose I want to get in better physical shape and therefore hire a personal trainer. The trainer and I meet and discuss my goals. We establish a plan that involves increasing my exercise regimen and changing my diet. For the first month, I follow the plan closely. The workouts are intense. My muscles are sore. My fridge is full of fruits and vegetables. My stomach wonders if candy bars have suddenly gone off the market entirely. It is a painful process of change, but I stick to it. I start to notice small increases in my stamina and small decreases in my weight. After a month, the trainer and I meet again. This time he says, "I've decided to change course. I don't want you to exercise at all. In fact, try not to even break a sweat. Go ahead and eat anything you want, as much as you want, at any time. If it feels good, do it. Don't worry about following any of the previous plans we had." I guarantee it would be much easier to follow such counsel than to stick to the original plan. But would such a turn of events be considered a "blessing" to me? Following the new plan would surely result in poorer physical health and decreased energy. That was not what I signed up for. Even though it would be easier in the short term, I know after time I would reflect on my lack of progress and be disappointed. Even though smooth sailing is pleasant, it does not help us grow nearly as much as the struggle that comes with rough seas.

Several of the gospel writers refer to a time when Jesus was with his disciples on the Sea of Galilee. This body of water is known to get violent storms of a sudden, and so it was the case during this particular New Testament account. "And behold, there arose a great tempest in the sea, insomuch that the ship was covered with waves: but he was asleep" (Matthew 8:24). "He" refers to Jesus Christ. Mark goes on to explain that the waves and winds were very treacherous, and the boat was filling with water (see Mark 4:37). Luke goes even further to state the entire vessel and party on board were in "jeopardy" (see Luke 8:23). Think about those who were on the boat. Many of the Savior's disciples were fisherman and likely experienced mariners. This storm seems to have been strong and intense enough that even these veteran sailors were concerned. Their level of distress continued to rise, to the point where they felt they would likely die. Matthew and Luke record how the disciples warned the Lord with the statement "we perish" (see Matthew 8:25 and Luke 8:24). Mark claims the cry for help was even more personal and perhaps even somewhat passive-aggressive, recording the petition as, "Master, carest thou not that we perish?" (Mark 4:38).

Why did the disciples need to make Jesus aware of the pending doom? Why would they go so far as to presume He somehow didn't care they were all going to die? *Because Jesus was asleep.* As the group frantically bailed water, tied things down, adjusted position, and did everything they could think of to keep from drowning, Jesus slept peacefully near the end of the ship. Waves crashed, winds roared, the boat took on gallon after gallon of water, and yet He slept. I'm sure this was a great curiosity to the apostles. Perhaps when they originally set out to sea, the waters were calm. The Savior was a hard worker and was subject to fatigue as other mortals. It appears He even found a pillow to sleep on (see Mark 4:38). At the outset, it was no surprise to the apostles to watch their Master rest. As the winds picked up, it probably didn't raise any concern either. Maybe the first drops of rain or the first wave that brought a little water into the boat lifted an apostolic eyebrow or two. Perhaps they commented among themselves, "Is He still sleeping? He must be really tired. I'm not sure I could sleep through this." As the storm intensified and the threat went from concerning to dangerous, their fear could only be matched with their bewilderment. "How can he continue to sleep? We are about to drown and yet He is apparently unaware and unconcerned." Maybe such thoughts are what prompted Mark's recording of the alert, suggesting the Savior somehow did not care that they were all going to die (see Mark 4:38).

Before we address why the Savior was able to sleep during the storm, let's consider the faithless nature of the disciples' plea. "Carest thou not that we perish" is a strong statement. Essentially it means, "We are about to die. You are sleeping. Apparently, you don't even care enough about us to get up and help us bail water or save this ship." This was an extreme mischaracterization of the Savior's intentions. Had they only realized how much He sacrificed to even come to earth; a God condescending to live like man, to suffer like His creations, and to endure their limited understanding. Had they understood the contents of the cup He would partake in years to come, which suffering caused even a God to "tremble because of pain" (D&C 19:18), perhaps they wouldn't have asked such a question. Elder Joseph B. Wirthlin eloquently elaborated this point: "At times we may be tempted to think the Savior is oblivious to our trials. In fact, the reverse is true; it is we who need to be awakened in our hearts to His teachings." [1] Jesus Christ's entire mission was to prevent them from perishing from physical and spiritual death. Yet their limited focus and immediate panic had them inappropriately questioning His motives. Their doubt would soon be resolved in dramatic fashion.

Let's get back to the scenario that prompted the disciples' doubt in the first place; how could the Savior sleep under such conditions? The answer is simple. If you believed you were going to suffer death by drowning in a spectacular storm, panic and fear would be an understandable reaction. However, if you knew there was no possible way you would die in that storm, that the worst that would happen is you'd get wet and have your nap interrupted, and that you could make the storm cease with a single command, how would you feel? I suppose the person who had such a thought process would feel quite calm and in control, and sleep would come easily. The Savior knew He was not going to drown. The manner of his death had been foretold for generations. He would be raised on the cross at Calvary, not one minute sooner or later than determined by heavenly design, and there and then He would voluntarily exit this mortal sphere. The Sea of Galilee posed no threat to his existence. After the disciples awoke Him, Jesus chastised them for their lack of faith. Then with a single command, the Lord of heaven and earth rebuked the storm. Immediately there was a great calm, which had to have been extremely shocking and impressive to the apostles. In reverent astonishment they remarked, "What manner of man is this, that even the winds and the sea obey him!" (Matthew 8:27).

This account contains a very important principle to help people manage anxiety. The principle is this: feelings are a product of the way we think. When we change how we think about and perceive our environment, we change the resultant feelings and emotions. The Savior and His apostles were in the exact same storm, in the same boat, in the same degree of potential peril. The only significant difference was the way in which they perceived their circumstances. The disciples thought

---

1 Joseph B. Wirthlin, "Finding a Safe Harbor," The Church of Jesus Christ of Latter-day Saints, May 2000, https://www.lds.org/ensign/2000/05/finding-a-safe-harbor?lang=eng.

they were going to die, and therefore felt anxiety. The Savior knew He would not die and could stop the storm anytime He chose, and therefore felt no anxiety.

There is a companion principle here that is also important to understand. The Savior did not *need* to calm the storm in order to sleep. With His understanding and knowledge of the truth, He was able to endure the tempest with peace of mind and heart. His peace was generated from within, regardless of the external circumstances. I have known many, many people throughout my life who try to reduce anxiety through the exact opposite process. Instead of changing the way they think about the storm, *they try to stop the storm.* They try to manage their external environment so completely as to eliminate all possibility they will experience anxiety. Most anyone would consider it foolish if they were on a boat and a storm began and their captain started barking commands such as, "You! Smooth out that wave! Make it smaller! You! Slow that wind down! Change its course!" It would be absurd. Yet this is what happens when we try to unreasonably control our environment. I see people working feverishly to ensure the house is spotless, the kids all have straight A's, children get first place in all sports tournaments, the church lessons are perfect, the image in the mirror looks ten years younger than actual age, and family pictures are filtered, cropped and processed to eliminate any evidence of possible imperfection. (I'll be honest; I got a little tired just *writing* that sentence.) Some think if everything is perfect and in order in their life, then they won't have to worry about outcomes. If we do everything just right, then nothing can go wrong. While I admire the grit and determination of those who work so hard every day to stop the waves and slow the wind, I grieve for their perpetually unsuccessful efforts. I am reminded of the legend of Sisyphus, who was banished to the underworld by Zeus. Sisyphus was tasked with rolling a giant boulder from the bottom of a hill to the top. However, each time he came close to finishing his task, the boulder would escape his control and roll back to the bottom, leaving him to start over. Trying to manage all external aspects of your life in order to reduce anxiety *does not work* and will leave you frustrated and fearful. Instead of trying to calm the storm, we should focus on navigating the boat. Put simply, we need to work on changing our thoughts and perceptions.

Anxiety is a part of life. It is a normal reaction to many issues. Excessive anxiety can become problematic but can also be effectively managed. We need to remember that "this life is the time for men to prepare to meet God" (Alma 34:32). We are not going to meet the measure of our creation if we do not go through trials and difficulties. If you struggle with anxiety, it could very well be part of your Father in Heaven's plan to help you learn and become stronger. Try not to view all challenges as something gone awry or amiss. Many challenges are heaven sent, and if managed well, will help us become something much better and more noble.

Practical suggestions for change:

Try to view anxiety as a stepping stone for growth as opposed to an impediment in your path.

Focus on changing your internal perspective instead of trying to change your circumstances.

CHAPTER TWO

You Are in Control

"For the power is in them, wherein they are agents unto themselves. And inasmuch as men do good they shall in nowise lose their reward." (D&C 58:28)

Emotions are a byproduct of the way we think about things, and anxiety is no exception. Anxiety is the natural reaction to a thought or perception. The psychological notion behind this model is called cognitive theory. Cognitive theory holds that emotions are driven by perceptions and mental patterns. The theory can be simply explained as follows:

We don't have complete control over the events that occur in our lives, so it makes little sense to try to intervene at the first step of the process. As discussed in the previous chapter, trying to manage the "event" stage is like trying to stop the storm. Just as storms happen, other events happen as well. There is only so much we can do about changing our daily events. When we try to change what happens to us, we often end up spending a lot of energy for very few results. Therefore, trying to change events is usually not effective. Trying to intervene at the "emotion" stage is fruitless, because it is a consequence of the first two steps. It is very difficult to simply "stop" feeling a certain way. So many times, our feelings seem to simply overwhelm our experience and we don't know how to make them go away. That leaves the second stage, "belief about event," as the most effective place for intervention. We *can* change the way we think about things. Here's an example of how our perceptions affect our emotions:

You wake up on Saturday morning and check the weather forecast. The forecast calls for steady rain all day. So, the "event" in our three-step process is a rainy day. How does that make you feel? Well, you could have any number of emotions depending on how you perceive things.

- If you are planning a 20-mile bike ride and hoping for sunshine, your emotion equals disappointment.
- If you are in the midst of selling your home, are under a strict time crunch, and need just one sunny Saturday in order to get essential things done, your emotion equals frustration.
- If you live in a flood zone and there had been consistent rain for several weeks, with forecasters warning that one more day of rain would require evacuations, your emotion equals high anxiety.
- If you are a farmer in a drought and have been praying for rain for weeks, your emotion equals relief.

In each case, the event is the same. Yet depending upon the way in which the event is perceived, the emotion is different. This can even happen "on the fly" so to speak. Let's say your son is late coming home from a date. He isn't answering his phone. The "event" is the lateness of his arrival. You start to think, "Something must be wrong. Perhaps he is hurt or was in an accident." The resulting emotion is fear and panic. Then five minutes later he calls and apologizes. Both the car battery and his phone battery died, and he had to jump start the car and then charge his phone in order to call. He will be home in five minutes. Your feelings of panic and fear immediately cease. The "event" of him arriving late is still there, but because you have more information you are able to perceive the situation differently. The point is, if you want to change your emotions, you need to change your thoughts first.

A scriptural example can illustrate this point as well. In approximately the ninth century B.C., the Syrian army went to war against

Israel. Elisha was a prophet at that time. The Syrian king had his battle plans foiled on several occasions and started to wonder whether one of his servants was a traitor, revealing information to Israel's armies. The king's confidants assured him none of them were confederate, but said, "Elisha, the prophet that is in Israel, telleth the king of Israel the words that thou speakest in thy bedchamber" (2 Kings 6:12). In other words, they said, "God is telling Elisha your plans, and then he's telling Israel's king." The king of Syria decided to put an end to this. He sent an army to surround Elisha's city. Elisha's servant arose early and discovered the pending siege, becoming duly frightened. He warned Elisha, stating, "Alas, my master! how shall we do?" (2 Kings 6:15). Elisha seemed unconcerned, despite the threat of hundreds of armed soldiers ready to break down his door and carry him away captive. Calmly, he counseled his servant: "Fear not: for they that be with us are more than they that be with them" (2 Kings 6:16). The servant was likely incredulous, for there was no way they could adequately defend themselves. Surely Elisha must have misjudged, as the enemy was considerably more numerous than they. Sensing the servant's anxiety, Elisha prayed, "Lord, I pray thee, open his eyes, that he may see. And the Lord opened the eyes of the young man; and he saw: and, behold, the mountain was full of horses and chariots of fire round about Elisha" (2 Kings 6:17). Contrary to the servant's former belief, Elisha and company were well defended by a numerous and powerful heavenly host. Both Elisha and his servant were in the same situation, but because Elisha knew something that changed his perception, his reaction was calm instead of fearful. As the servant developed the same perspective, his reaction surely changed as well. *As we change the way we think about things, we change the way we feel about things.*

Some will say, "I don't know how to change my thoughts. I'm not even aware of them. Something will happen, and I immediately start to have anxiety. It's not like I consciously go through a thought process and then get anxious; it just happens." I completely agree with that explanation. Cognition happens very quickly, usually beyond our awareness. The brain is very efficient. It does not require us to consciously think about behaviors and thought patterns that have become routine. If I'm going to stand up from a seated position, I don't have to intentionally think to put both feet down, lean forward, press my legs into the floor, and raise my body. Even though the brain gives the command for each of these steps to happen, the process has become so automatic that it doesn't require conscious input.

In addition, you don't need to fully understand a process in order to make it happen. Think about driving a car. There are very complicated mechanisms that control acceleration and braking. Some people know exactly how these mechanisms function, down to the individual steps. Most people have no idea how it works, but they know if you press on the gas pedal you'll likely move forward, and if you hit the brakes you'll likely slow down. Our perceptions are formed over very long periods of time, influenced by multiple experiences. In fact, our perceptions are constantly being modified by daily input. Just like driving your car, you don't need to understand everything about your perceptions in order to modify them. You'll need some insight into your behavior and thinking patterns and why you do certain things, but that can usually be achieved without a deep understanding of every aspect of who you are.

Perceptions are not permanent. Because of the way the brain works, perceptions that have been held for a long time become resistant to casual efforts to change them. However, any perception can be changed if sufficient time and effort is applied. Sometimes when we fail to make lasting change even after strong effort, we blame the process. There are times when we truly desire to change a certain pattern of thought or behavior. Some of these patterns we have held for decades. I've worked with people with anxiety issues and given them strategies to help manage anxiety. Some of them come back a week later and tell me, "I did what you told me, and I still have anxiety. Your methods don't work." They are frustrated and blame the system instead of their efforts. As compassionately as possible, I try to help them understand how a 30-year pattern is not going to change with one week of effort. We have to apply new principles and new styles of thinking over and over and over again, for months and sometimes years, before we start to see real and lasting change. It is very hard work that is fraught with setbacks and frustration. However, it can work every time when done correctly and consistently.

Feeling as if you have no control is very different from actually having no control. Satan would have us believe we do not have control over our situation, thus trying to nurture feelings of hopelessness. Indeed, trying and failing repeatedly can be quite frustrating. However, this can be part of a divine plan for change if we can effectively manage our attitude. Let's consider two contrasting stories from the Book of Mormon, both involving groups fighting for their freedom.

The people of King Limhi were in bondage to the Lamanites. These were the same people who had lived under the reign of wicked King Noah. They had followed King Noah's poor example and had become sinful. The Lord sent Abinadi the prophet to warn them of their iniquities and command them to repent. Abinadi told them if they did not repent they would be brought into bondage. The people did not listen to Abinadi and he was martyred. Eventually the prophecy came true and the people were captured by the Lamanites. They lived in captivity for several years, being subjected to hard labor and cruel conditions. The people determined they had endured enough and decided to go to war to free themselves. They went to battle and were defeated by the Lamanites. The scriptures record that they became angry after their first loss and prepared for another battle. The second battle resulted in another significant loss, which angered them even further. A third time they went to defeat their foes and be liberated from their servitude. "Yea, they went again even the third time, and suffered in the like manner; and those that were not slain returned again to the city of Nephi. And they did humble themselves even to the dust, subjecting themselves to the yoke of bondage, submitting themselves to be smitten, and to be driven to and fro, and burdened, according to the desires of their enemies. And they did humble themselves even in the depths of humility; and they did cry mightily to God; yea, even all the day long did they cry unto their God that he would deliver them out of their afflictions" (Mosiah 21:12-14). After being sorely defeated for the third time, they humbled themselves and submitted their will to God.

Hundreds of years later, the Nephite nation was at the height of wickedness and under attack from the Lamanites. Mormon, the same who abridged the Book of Mormon, was their military leader at the time. Many years prior, Samuel the Lamanite had prophesied if the

Nephites did not repent of their sins, the time would come that their land would be overrun with thieves. It would become so severe that robberies and thefts would be a constant threat. This prophecy came true among the Nephites during the time of Mormon. Mormon, who remained righteous, commented on the attitude of the Nephites as their condition worsened: "And it came to pass that the Nephites began to repent of their iniquity, and began to cry even as had been prophesied by Samuel the prophet.... And it came to pass that when I, Mormon, saw their lamentation and their mourning and their sorrow before the Lord, my heart did begin to rejoice within me, knowing the mercies and the long-suffering of the Lord, therefore supposing that he would be merciful unto them that they would again become a righteous people" (Mormon 2:10,12). Mormon was hopeful that their sufferings would help them be humble, that they would turn to God and truly repent of their wrongdoings. However, Mormon was disappointed in his hope, and reported, "But behold this my joy was vain, for their sorrowing was not unto repentance, because of the goodness of God; but it was rather the sorrowing of the damned, because the Lord would not always suffer them to take happiness in sin. And they did not come unto Jesus with broken hearts and contrite spirits, but they did curse God, and wish to die. Nevertheless they would struggle with the sword for their lives" (Mormon 2:13-14). Even despite their situation being dire, the Nephites did not humble themselves, but became more entrenched in their anger and sinful ways. Mormon goes on to describe the pitiful scene of thousands upon thousands of men and women "hewn down in open rebellion against their God and heaped up as dung upon the face of the land" (Mormon 2:15). The imagery is somewhat shocking.

Here we have two groups in similar situations. Both are under attack by their enemies. Both are fighting for their lives. Both are failing in their attempts. Yet the first group, the people of King Limhi, responded to their suffering with humility and a desire to repent. The second group, Mormon's cohorts, responded to their suffering with anger, rage, and a refusal to return to God. King Limhi's people were eventually freed from bondage. Mormon's people were eventually completely exterminated.

From this example, we learn that repeated trials met with repeated failures can yield very different results, depending upon attitude. Failure will almost inevitably lead to feelings of disappointment. At that point, there is usually a fork in the road. One path leads to humility and acceptance, generating fertile ground for change. The other path leads to anger and frustration, halting forward movement. If you have struggled with anxiety for years and years, with your efforts to change yielding no noticeable differences, where are you on this path? Surely you have already passed through the disappointment of failure; are you on the path of humility or the path of anger? Do you still believe you can change through the Atonement of Jesus Christ, or have you accepted the lie that you are beyond hope? Such lies originate from Lucifer. Elder Richard G. Scott warned against Satan's clever ways. "Lucifer will do all in his power to keep you captive. You are familiar with his strategy. He whispers: 'No one will ever know.' 'Just one more time.' 'You can't change; you have tried before and failed.' 'It's too late; you've gone too far.' Don't let him discourage you." [2] Don't believe the adversary's deceptions. *Change is always possible, as long as we desire and work for it.* When we stop trying to change, for whatever reason, our eternal progress becomes frustrated.

We have been given the marvelous gift of agency. Agency is the ability to make choices for ourselves. Specifically, it is the privilege of choosing between good and evil. As we have already noted, being able to choose *and* being enticed by one choice or another is essential to our mortal development. Knowing of the critical nature of agency, Satan has sought to eliminate it. From the beginning, Satan tried to take away our choices and force us to choose according to his desires. "And I, the Lord God, spake unto Moses, saying: That Satan, whom thou hast commanded in the name of mine Only Begotten, is the same which was from the beginning, and he came before me, saying—Behold, here am I, send me, I will be thy son, and I will redeem all mankind, that one soul shall not be lost, and surely I will do it; wherefore give me thine honor" (Moses 4:1). In order to ensure no souls would be lost and all would return to heaven, Satan proposed to strip us of our ability

2 Richard G. Scott, "Finding the Way Back", The Church of Jesus Christ of Latter-day Saints, May 1990, https://www.lds.org/ensign/1990/05/finding-the-way-back?lang=eng.

to choose. We would not sin because we would have no voice in the matter. Clearly, he failed to understand how returning to Father in Heaven is not simply a matter of walking a straight line. We have to *choose* to walk the straight line, while being tempted to deviate, so we can develop the strength and character to not only return to God but be like Him as well.

Because of agency, we have a natural and good desire to want to be free. Generally speaking, we don't like being told what to do or having something forced upon us. This seems evident from a young age and continues throughout the lifespan. Babies don't like having their mouths wiped clean. Adolescents don't like having a curfew. Adults don't like having an overbearing employer. Seniors don't like being moved from their own home to a retirement community. Indeed, nations have been born from the collective desire of individuals to have autonomy and make their own choices. This desire comes from God and the resultant autonomy is a gift from the Savior. "And the Messiah cometh in the fulness of time, that he may redeem the children of men from the fall. And because that they are redeemed from the fall they have become free forever, knowing good from evil; *to act for themselves and not to be acted upon*, save it be by the punishment of the law at the great and last day, according to the commandments which God hath given" (2 Nephi 2:26, emphasis added).

"To act for themselves and not be acted upon" is an important statement and reflects the core of the concept previously noted. Because of the redemption we are no longer slaves to sin but can choose our own outcome on the conditions of repentance. We are in control of our own choices. In most areas we all tend to agree with this truth. Yet I have noticed a disturbing trend regarding this issue as it relates to our perceptions of mental health problems. For generations, mental health concerns were considered shameful and not often discussed. People typically did not reach out for help, and these problems went untreated. Thankfully those times changed many years ago, and it became appropriate and understandable to seek professional mental health assistance. However, in the last decade or so I have seen the pendulum continue to swing. More and more I deal with people who not only acknowledge the fact they have mental health issues, but also seem to embrace such issues and incorporate them as part of their identity. Often they have dealt with these concerns for many years. When we visit, they say, "My anxiety has been going on for as long as I can remember, and I can't control it." Although it may be pure semantics, I find it very interesting when people refer to mental health issues with the possessive "*my*." To me that suggests a high degree of internalization and perhaps even hopeless acceptance of the condition. I believe there is a large difference between "my anxiety has been present for ten years" and "Ten years ago I was diagnosed with an anxiety disorder." For some people, it seems when they say "my anxiety" they are also stating "this is a condition that is an unchangeable part of me; there's nothing I can do about it." Such individuals may be less likely to seek change due to feelings of helplessness. I fear our society has reached a point where many feel anxiety issues are permanent and beyond their capacity to change. I do not believe such perceptions are true. Change is always possible.

Accepting the truth that we have weakness is an important part of growth and personal development. That acceptance is often the starting point for many people. However, when we believe our weakness cannot be changed, we fall prey to one of Satan's deceptions. He would have us believe that certain things about our personality cannot be changed. The "hopeless acceptance" of mental health conditions seems to be part of this deception. Perhaps it is similar to a "if you can't beat them, join them" sort of strategy. Those who have struggled with anxiety for so long and suffered many failed attempts at change appear to throw up their hands in surrender and believe it's a permanent condition. I understand the frustrations shared by so many who, despite ongoing efforts, have not found success. In no way do I mean to make light of this circumstance. However, I do propose this style of thinking is mistaken. Having no hope for change is a perfect recipe to remain stuck in our current situation. To me, that sounds more like Satan's lies than the truths of the Spirit. Satan tells us we cannot change, we shouldn't try, and our efforts will result in failure once more. The Spirit whispers, "Keep trying, you will eventually succeed; be patient in your afflictions."

We should not become victims of our own thoughts and perceptions. We need to "act" to change the way we perceive things and not "be acted upon" by old patterns and incorrect assumptions. The process of change I'm suggesting is not easy but is very, very possible. Believing it is possible is absolutely essential to beginning the process of change. If we believe we cannot change certain things, including feelings of anxiety, change will become less and less likely as our hope fades. Choose to believe you can make a difference in your life. Choose to believe that perhaps there are strategies you haven't tried or lessons you have yet to learn. Choose to believe the Savior helps all who come unto Him, and in His good time He will give mercifully to all who ask in faith.

Practical suggestions for change:

Understand that feelings are a product of the way we think. As we change our thinking we can change the way we feel.

Believe that you can change the way you think, through a combination of your own efforts and the help provided from your Heavenly Father.

CHAPTER THREE:

Developing Personal Power Through the Atonement of Jesus Christ

"For it is expedient that an atonement should be made; for according to the great plan of the Eternal God there must be an atonement made, or else all mankind must unavoidably perish; yea, all are hardened; yea, all are fallen and are lost, and must perish except it be through the atonement which it is expedient should be made." (Alma 34:9)

As Adam and Eve chose to partake of the fruit of the tree of knowledge of good and evil, they also accepted the associated consequence: "thou shalt surely die" (Moses 3:17). Two types of death fell upon Adam and Eve that day. First, their bodies were transformed to a physical and corruptible state. As surely as they had been created, the day would come that they would die. Their spirits would leave their bodies with no promise of reunification. We refer to this consequence as physical death. All the posterity of Adam and Eve, born into the fallen world they chose to enter, are subject to physical death. Second, they were cast out of the Garden of Eden and removed from the presence of God. They could hear His voice coming from the garden but could not enjoy His company (see Moses 5:4). The separation of man from God is called spiritual death. It comes upon all who sin and therefore become ineligible to return to the presence of the Father, as no unclean thing can dwell with God (see 1 Nephi 10:21).

What was mankind to do? While they would all receive physical bodies, the same bodies would be taken from them upon death. Despite a strong desire, they would never be able to return to their loving heavenly home because of sinful choices that befall all mortals. In the preexistence we admired and revered our Father in Heaven. Not only did He have a body of flesh and bone, but He had achieved perfection. As His children and heirs, we wanted to be like Him in every way. The Fall of Adam would apparently derail our plans and make us forever subject to the will of Lucifer.

Yet in His infinite wisdom, Heavenly Father had foreseen Adam and Eve's transgression and made appropriate arrangements. Not only did the plan of salvation include our receiving mortal bodies and coming to Earth for a period of testing and trial, it contained a full contingency plan for our rescue should we go off course. No wonder the "morning stars sang together, and the sons of God shouted for joy" when the great plan of happiness was presented (Job 38:7). Jehovah would assume the role of Savior and Redeemer, providing escape from the effects of physical and spiritual death. The consequence of physical death is upon all born into mortality, regardless of their choices. Appropriately, the reversal of physical death is gifted to all born into mortality, regardless of their choices. The power of the resurrection will reunite body and spirit for all, as Amulek taught: "Now, this restoration shall come to all, both old and young, both bond and free, both male and female, both the wicked and the righteous; and even there shall not so much as a hair of their heads be lost; but every thing shall be restored to its perfect frame, as it is now, or in the body, and shall be brought and be arraigned before the bar of Christ the Son, and God the Father, and the Holy Spirit, which is one Eternal God, to be judged according to their works, whether they be good or whether they be evil" (Alma 11:44).

Spiritual death comes as the result of sin. We separate ourselves from God as we choose to disobey His commandments. Little children are born into this world in a perfect, sinless state. They are unable to sin until they reach eight years of age, the age of accountability (see Moroni 8:8-12). At that time, they have the choice to be baptized and receive the gift of the Holy Ghost, which fully purifies once again. I suppose if a newly baptized eight-year-old could go his whole life without committing a sin, he might not be subject to spiritual death. I remember having similar thoughts after my baptism. As I came up out of the water and was subsequently confirmed, I felt clean and pure. I thought to myself, "I'm never going to sin again!" As I recall, my resolution lasted for about ten minutes, my cleanliness ending with teasing and arguing with my younger sister on the way home. Alas, I became subject to spiritual death. Fortunately, the gift of repentance is available to all as well. However, it is not an unconditional, "no strings attached" gift like the resurrection. Dying is not our fault. Sinning *is* our fault. As a result, repentance becomes an individual experience predicated on certain conditions. All who sin can seek repentance. If they are able to meet the demands set by the Savior, forgiveness is granted. Such forgiveness is complete. It does not come with an asterisk or annotation. Elder Dale G. Renlund, quoting President Boyd K. Packer, made the following statement: "The Atonement leaves no tracks, no traces. What it fixes is fixed. ... It just heals, and what it heals stays healed. The Atonement, which can reclaim each one of us, bears no scars. That means that no matter what we have done or where we have been or how something happened, if we truly repent, [the Savior] has promised that He would atone. And when He atoned, that settled that. ...The Atonement ... can wash clean every stain no matter how difficult or how long or how many times repeated." [3]

What does repentance and the Atonement of Jesus Christ have to do with the management of anxiety? Please believe me when I tell you repentance and the Atonement of Jesus Christ has *everything* to do with *any* change we make in our lives. Some will say, "Yes, I know that Jesus can help me change. But this is different. I'm not talking about being more righteous or trying to do my church assignment better. I'm talking about dealing with mental health issues. I'm talking about trying to control anxiety." I have heard that logic many times as I have introduced the idea of gospel solutions to mental health issues. Let's dissect the argument with spiritual truth. First, there is nothing truly "physical," for all things are spiritual to God (see D&C 29:34). Our nature is truly spiritual. All of our mortal experiences contribute to our spiritual development. I promise your Father in Heaven is truly invested in helping you resolve those issues that will increase your spiritual power and ease your emotional suffering. Second, repentance *is* the agent of change in our lives. It is not simply being cleansed from

3 Dale G. Renlund, "Repentance: A Joyful Choice," *Ensign*, November 2016, 122.

sin; it is the process by which we become more like God. Using a broad definition, "sin" could be considered *anything* that makes us different from God, whether it be evil desires or untoward personal character traits.

Some of you will remember the era of "decorative bathroom soaps." For those of you less seasoned with age, I will describe. These were molded, hard soaps that came in various shapes. Some of them were quite lovely and served as a sort of centerpiece for home bathrooms. I recall being a young boy and spending time at my grandparents' home. They had these soaps in their bathroom; one of them was in the shape of a seashell. I came in from playing outside and went to the bathroom to wash my hands. My mother was with me. As I reached for the seashell soap, she said, "David, stop! Don't use that soap." She opened a bathroom drawer and pulled out a dingy block of regular soap. "Use this one," she said. I learned quickly that the decorative soaps were not to be used, but were to be left intact, looking beautiful and smelling delightful. Years later I recall visiting another home and saw similar soaps in the bathroom. They were covered in shrink-wrapped plastic. Please take a minute and think about that last sentence: *the soaps were covered in plastic.* What possible good can a soap do if it is wrapped in plastic? All it is good for is to be admired. It will never get dirty or misshapen, but at the same time its primary use has been completely stripped away. Statues are made to be admired and looked at; soap is made to remove dirt. Somebody must have seen the folly in this because I don't see a lot of decorative bath soaps any longer.

I am concerned that some view the Atonement of Jesus Christ and repentance as a sort of plastic-coated soap decoration. "Repentance? Oh yes, we have it. It's right here in our bathroom in a little dish. It's wrapped safely in plastic. Isn't is beautiful? Of course, we never want to have to use it. We plan on living our lives just right, so we don't have to open the soap. You never have to wash a hand that never gets dirty, you know..." Considering the terrible price paid by our Savior in Gethsemane and on Golgotha, I don't think He ever intended repentance to be used sparingly. It is not to be admired as a quaint gift but to be used as a daily cleanser. Lucifer is the author of the "decorative soap" version of repentance. He wants you to believe you can make it through life without help. He wants you to believe that admitting weakness is wrong. He wants you to believe repentance is for "big sins" and not for everyday change. Remember, *he is a liar*. He is bent on your destruction and misery (see 2 Nephi 2:27). Anytime you change for the better, I believe you are utilizing the process of repentance. President Russell M. Nelson said, "The doctrine of repentance is much broader than a dictionary's definition…when Jesus said "repent," He asked us to change—to change our mind, knowledge, and spirit…the Lord has commanded us to repent, to change our ways, to come unto Him, and be more like Him." [4]

Repentance is the process by which we go from our fallen state to become like our Father in Heaven. We discussed previously how God's purpose is for us to achieve eternal life, which is to be like Him and live like Him (see Moses 1:39). If this is God's purpose, surely it should be our purpose as well. Men and women were created in the image of our heavenly parents. Our similarities were not intended to end with the physical likeness. One of the main purposes of this life is to go through a process of personal and spiritual refinement, where we eliminate all worldly aspects of our personalities and acquire the characteristics that God Himself possesses. I do not believe celestial beings experience feelings such as worry, depression, anxiety or anything similar. I believe their attitude is one of confidence, security, and full control of the situation. In order for us to develop comparable natures, we need to learn to manage anxiety, depression, poor self-esteem, or any characteristic or liability that makes us different from God.

In the previous chapter we briefly discussed the idea of a societal tendency to view mental health issues as unchangeable. I'd like to revisit this in greater depth and from a slightly different angle. As previously discussed, psychological problems have been viewed as shameful for decades, often not discussed. People with mild to moderate emotional issues simply did not talk about them, and people with significant challenges were shuttered away in terrible facilities. Over time society became more willing to address these problems. People started to slowly acknowledge mental health concerns. Resources such as counseling and

4 Russell M. Nelson, "Repentance and Conversion," *Ensign*, May 2007, 103.

pharmaceuticals became mainstream to the benefit of everyone. The collective societal attitude of "we don't talk about mental health issues" gave way to "let's talk about mental health issues and do something to fix them." This is a positive change that has provided help to millions around the world. Yet most recently, perhaps in the past five years, I have seen the pendulum continue to swing. More and more I see individuals and groups who are not only willing to accept mental health issues but perceive and promote them as unchangeable. A personal example will help illustrate the point.

My wife, Kristyn, and I are the parents of six children. For those of you who have children, you know they do not always sleep through the night, especially when they are infants. Kristyn and I would take turns getting up at night for feedings and other necessities. As I would get up to tend to the babies over the years, I developed of habit of eating a snack as well. Due to a chronic sweet tooth, my snack was usually a dessert, such as a cookie or piece of cake. Six children and about a decade of nighttime feedings later, I had developed my own "nighttime feeding" habit. We were thrilled when our youngest child finally started sleeping through the night on a regular basis. However, I was not sleeping through the night. I had acquired a pattern of behavior where I would get up in the middle of the night and eat a treat. This pattern endured for many years. *I hated it.* I felt so weak. Each night I would go to bed and tell myself, "I'm not going to get up and eat tonight." Yet each night the pattern would be the same. I'd wake up around 2:00 a.m., sit up and think, "Hmmm. Feels about time for a snack." The snack always tasted delicious in the midnight hours. That same snack sat like a toxic lump in my stomach in the morning. In addition to having stomach cramps upon waking in the morning, I had a feeling of failure.

This problem would often become a topic of discussion in our marriage. I would comment on my perceived lack of willpower and feelings of inadequacy. My wife, who is better than me in just about everything, was always trying to find solutions and suggestions to help me beat the habit. At one point she suggested, "Why don't you just embrace the fact you are a nighttime eater? Instead of fighting it, accept it as part of who you are?" I know she meant well and was perhaps hoping a bit of reverse psychology would work on the psychologist himself. But the idea of giving in to this terrible habit did not appeal to me in the least. I did not want to be that person. I did not like the way it made me feel and I wanted to find the path to change. I'm happy to report I've made considerable progress in eliminating my nighttime eating habit, although it is still a struggle at times.

Accepting we are flawed is a crucial step in repentance and change. *Giving in and surrendering to our flaws can stop the change process dead in its tracks.* I hope the distinction between these two statements is clear, because it makes the difference between hope and despair. I didn't want to be a "nighttime eater." I didn't want to accept that flaw as part of my personality, apparently resistant to any hope of change. With the shift in perception of mental health issues, some people view emotional challenges as things that 1) cannot be changed, 2) should be accepted as such, and 3) should not be challenged. Using anxiety as an example, let's compare how the approach has changed over time:

> 1950s approach to mental health issues: We don't talk about it. We don't acknowledge it. If it gets too severe, we'll hide it away.
>
> 1990s approach to mental health issues: Let's talk about it. Let's acknowledge it. If it gets too severe, let's treat it. It might be painful and difficult to change, but here are the tools.
>
> 2018 approach to mental health issues: Let's talk about it. Let's acknowledge it. If it gets too severe, don't worry. It's just the way you are. Instead of you trying to change something that doesn't seem to want to change, we'll ask society to change so you don't have to be so uncomfortable.

I feel strongly about this topic. I also want to tread lightly because I know that many who read this are part of that group who feel they cannot change. They feel anxiety is simply a part of their personalities that will never go away. Just as my wife was trying to help my nighttime eating habits with the suggestion to accept and embrace my negative behavior, I think society is trying to help those with chronic mental health issues by encouraging them to accept and embrace their challenges. It is a sympathetic approach that means very well. However, in the end it is a damning process that results in spiritual and emotional stagnation.

From the foundations of this world, Satan has sought to overthrow the plan of Father in Heaven. The crux of his attack was to eliminate agency. "Wherefore, because that Satan rebelled against me, *and sought to destroy the agency of man*, which I, the Lord God, had given him, and also, that I should give unto him mine own power; by the power of mine Only Begotten, I caused that he should be cast down" (Moses 4:3, emphasis added). Satan fought in heaven and started a war. He was defeated. Satan tempted the Savior directly during His mortal ministry, trying to get him to sin and therefore become ineligible to be the Lamb without blemish (see Matthew 4:1-11). He was again defeated. While in the garden and on the cross, Jesus was subjected to every terror and suffering that Hell could possibly imagine. Surely Lucifer hoped the Son of God would crumble under such pressure. A failed effort to atone would spell eternal damnation for all of God's children. Yet the Savior persisted and succeeded. The magnificent Atonement of Jesus Christ was complete. It now stands forever, impervious from attack and ready to provide the means of salvation to all who will reach out in faith.

For as misled as Satan is, he sure is persistent. If you think he threw up his hands on that first Easter morn and said, "Well, I gave it a good shot. I guess I lost. It's time to hang up the pitchfork," you'd be wrong. His efforts have not ceased but have become more and more sophisticated. Although he cannot defeat the Atonement of Jesus Christ as a whole, he can seek to limit its redeeming power on an individual basis. Suppose you were asked to complete a task that required a certain tool. The task is very daunting and would be impossible without the use of the tool. But the tool is provided, along with instructions on how to use it. All that remains is your effort. Along comes a charismatic individual who engages you in the following discussion:

Satan: "How's it going?"

You: "Oh, pretty well. I have this project I'm trying to complete."

Satan: "I see. It looks very difficult."

You: "Man, you're not kidding. It's probably the most difficult project I've ever had. But I have this tool to help me. My boss said if

I keep using the tool correctly, then I'll be able to finish the project."

Satan: "That's interesting. Does the tool work?"

You: "I guess so, for the most part. But there are times when I don't seem to be making any progress at all. It gets frustrating. I want to believe the tool works, and I believe my boss when he says it does, but in practice, real progress is hard to come by."

Satan: "I've been around for a very long time. I've seen countless people working on similar projects with this so-called tool. All of them say the same thing you just did. Progress is slow. Sometimes it even seems like they are going *backward* instead of forward. Have you ever considered the fact you might not be able to finish this project? Perhaps the project is just too difficult? I'm not trying to insult you, but I hate to see people invest so much energy in tasks that simply cannot be completed."

You: "You make a good point. Sometimes I really do think that I cannot complete this project, even with the tool. I know the boss has faith in me, but maybe he doesn't truly understand my specific situation. I've got a lot going on right now in my life and tackling this project seems like a futile task."

Satan: "I think you may be right. It's not you, *the project is just too hard.* The boss should have never asked you to take on such a task. Why don't you quit working so hard with no results? Take a break for a while. Come on over and have a seat. I'd be happy to hold the tool while you rest…"

In grand or small scale, I have seen this situation play out almost *every single day* in the lives of those around me. Of course, we are the workers, the project is some aspect of personal change, the boss is our Father in Heaven, and the tool is the Atonement of Jesus Christ. Satan cannot eliminate the tool. He tried to do this and failed. Yet if he can get us to lay the tool down and quit using it, hasn't he achieved a measure of victory? If he can convince people that the Atonement of Jesus Christ simply will not work for them, to one degree or another, then in effect he has eliminated the power of that gift in the lives of those who choose not to use it. A tool on the shelf is like molded soap wrapped in plastic. It looks great but has zero utility until it is used for the intended purpose.

This is the heart of my concern. I am worried that society, with good intentions, has convinced many that their mental health issues are beyond change and should just be accepted as part of who they are. This is truly a full-blown attack on the Atonement of Jesus Christ and a frontal assault on our agency. As we have already reviewed, Satan "sought to destroy the agency of man" (Moses 4:3). Clearly his intention has not changed, and his efforts have not ceased. If he can get us to believe that certain things are beyond change and should be accepted, he has succeeded in limiting the power of the Redemption in our lives. By our own flawed thinking we have, in effect, destroyed our own agency. This was Satan's goal from the beginning.

Sometimes change can be elusive, for any number of reasons. There are times we don't see results because we are not properly motivated for change. Other times we don't have the correct tools. Sometimes we have the right tool but haven't developed sufficient mastery of use. Perhaps we are competent at using the tool but haven't used it long enough. Even then, sometimes we are blessed with challenges that may never completely resolve, that are designed for our growth and development. I don't like the idea of laboring at a task that might never be truly complete. If we see the goal as the completion of the task, we will become quite frustrated. However, *if the goal was never to complete the task but was to develop strength through the struggle*, then that changes our perspective. Reaching the elusive finish line ceases to be the goal. Instead, the goal becomes daily progress. I'm suggesting there may be much more sophisticated and heavenly purposes behind our emotional challenges than we had previously considered. Truly taught the prophet Isaiah, "For my thoughts are not your thoughts, neither are your ways my ways, saith the Lord. For as the heavens are higher than the earth, so are my ways higher than your ways, and my thoughts than your thoughts" (Isaiah 55:8-9).

I want everyone who reads this to begin the process of trading despair for hope. When it comes to any aspect of personal change, including the effective management of anxiety, the Atonement of Jesus Christ is the key. Revelation will direct us to scriptural insights, righteous behaviors, and appropriate professional resources that will help provide the means for change and growth. *The task is not easy.* It was never intended to be. We are here to change from fallen creatures, "carnal, sensual and devilish" (Moses 5:13), to beings who have attained "the measure of the stature of the fulness of Christ" (Ephesians 4:13). This process is daunting at best, but *completely possible* as we partner with the Savior and utilize the incredible and transformative power of the Atonement of Jesus Christ.

Practical suggestions for change:

Increase your understanding of the Atonement of Jesus Christ through study and prayer.

Accept the fact that you will never be given a challenge you cannot eventually conquer when you combine your efforts with the power of God.

CHAPTER FOUR

Jacob: An Anxiety Case Study

"Behold, my beloved brethren, I, Jacob, having been called of God, and ordained after the manner of his holy order, and having been consecrated by my brother Nephi, unto whom ye look as a king or a protector, and on whom ye depend for safety, behold ye know that I have spoken unto you exceedingly many things. Nevertheless, I speak unto you again; for I am desirous for the welfare of your souls. Yea, mine anxiety is great for you; and ye yourselves know that it ever has been." (2 Nephi 6:2-3)

Jacob was the son of Lehi and Sariah and the younger brother of the prophet Nephi. His life was somewhat different from that of his older siblings. In earlier years, Lehi and family lived in Jerusalem. They apparently enjoyed a very comfortable lifestyle as Lehi was considerably wealthy. Laman and Lemuel regularly lamented the fact they had to leave Jerusalem. As if leaving Jerusalem wasn't bad enough, Lehi's family was plunged into a years-long exodus through the desert. They had to hunt for their food and then eat it raw. They had to build things with their own hands. The women gave birth to children under these difficult circumstances. In addition to these trials, there was great animosity among the older children. The conflicts were so significant they reached murderous intent on multiple occasions. It was in these circumstances that Jacob was born. He never knew the comforts of Jerusalem, but only the wilderness, the sea, and an untamed land that was the setting for an ongoing civil war within his own family.

That's not much of a foundation on which to build a solid sense of self or stable emotional groundwork. In fact, anxiety is a common reaction to being exposed to regular chaos. We have a hard time trusting in a secure future when things that should be stable are in flux.

Such appeared to be Jacob's experience. He is credited with authoring twelve chapters in the Book of Mormon (2 Nephi 6 through 10; Jacob 1 through 7). In these chapters, Jacob specifically refers to his anxious feelings on four occasions:

"Nevertheless, I speak unto you again; for I am desirous for the welfare of your souls. Yea, *mine anxiety is great for you*; and ye yourselves know that it ever has been." (2 Nephi 6:3; emphasis added)

"For because of faith and great anxiety, it truly had been made manifest unto us concerning our people, what things should happen unto them." (Jacob 1:5; emphasis added)

"And ye yourselves know that I have hitherto been diligent in the office of my calling; *but I this day am weighed down with much more desire and anxiety* for the welfare of your souls than I have hitherto been." (Jacob 2:3; emphasis added)

"Behold, my beloved brethren, I will unfold this mystery unto you; if I do not, by any means, get shaken from my firmness in the Spirit, and stumble *because of my over anxiety for you*." (Jacob 4:18; emphasis added)

I think we can reasonably conclude Jacob had significant feelings of anxiety. Specifically, in Jacob 4:18, he refers to the possibility of being "shaken from firmness in the Spirit" because of his "over anxiety." To me that suggests a certain degree of struggle and conflict. It also suggests a possible concern that Jacob worried about how his anxious feelings would impact his spiritual development. I believe there are many throughout the world who can empathize with Jacob's experience.

In his parting counsel to his son, Lehi almost sounds apologetic as he refers to the trials of Jacob's younger years: "And now, Jacob, I speak unto you: Thou art my firstborn in the days of my tribulation in the wilderness. And behold, in thy childhood thou hast suffered afflictions and much sorrow, because of the rudeness of thy brethren. Nevertheless, Jacob, my firstborn in the wilderness, thou knowest the greatness of God; and he shall consecrate thine afflictions for thy gain" (2 Nephi 2:1-2). Lehi's simple and profound wisdom, expressed in other words, might have sounded something like this:

"Jacob, you've had a rough start to your life. I'm sorry for that.

Laman and Lemuel have caused us all a considerable amount of grief. You shouldn't have had to go through such difficulties at such a young age. Yet looking back doesn't do us a whole lot of good; we need to look forward and grow from our challenges. I know with certainty that your Father in Heaven will use these experiences to help you become stronger and more capable. Believe it or not, the day will come when you will look back with gratitude on the struggles of your early life."

Jacob goes on to lead the people as a powerful prophet. He preached significant gospel doctrine in the few chapters he wrote. It appears he had finished his writings in Jacob chapter six, as the final verse bids farewell to all (see Jacob 6:13). Then comes chapter seven, the actual final chapter of Jacob's writings. Jacob had a noteworthy confrontation with Sherem, a wicked and deceitful man. It would appear this experience was so significant that Jacob could not exclude it from the record. This concluding chapter of his Book of Mormon writings contains the story of their confrontation. Sherem's intentions were to lead people to believe there was no Christ and to shake them from their faith (see Jacob 7:2-3). Jacob comments on this, stating, "And he [Sherem] had hope to shake me from the faith, notwithstanding the many revelations and the many things which I had seen concerning these things; for I truly had seen angels, and they had ministered unto me. And also, I had heard the voice of the Lord speaking unto me in very word, from time to time; wherefore, *I could not be shaken*" (Jacob 7:5, emphasis added).

I find Jacob's statement very interesting. At some previous time in his life, he was worried he would be "shaken from his firmness in the spirit" due to his anxiety (Jacob 4:18). Yet at this later season, he makes a specific reference that he could *not* be shaken. What happened between his first statement which communicated fears of faltering and his second statement which was bold and unyielding? What was he able to do to calm his fears and develop greater confidence? I truly do not know the exact answer to that question. However, there are principles in Jacob's writings that give some clues as to what he believed and how he lived his life. I believe there are patterns we can follow that will help decrease our anxiety and fear and increase our feelings of faith. Let's consider some of these truths.

Principle #1: Be appropriately accountable

"And we did magnify our office unto the Lord, taking upon us the responsibility, answering the sins of the people upon our own heads if we did not teach them the word of God with all diligence; wherefore, by laboring with our might their blood might not come upon our garments; otherwise their blood would come upon our garments, and we would not be found spotless at the last day." (Jacob 1:19)

The first principle is to be accountable for *your* responsibilities. This can be a balancing act. We often tend to go too far in one direction or another. Some have difficulty taking accountability for themselves and their own decisions. Others take on too much responsibility, feeling they are to blame for the poor decisions of others. We have to find the right balance, where we are taking care of what is truly ours but not holding ourselves accountable for things outside of our control. When I was studying to be a psychologist I had to get some practical experience. The university provided options for internships. I took a position at a local counseling center. I distinctly remember the first actual client I visited with. She was about thirteen years of age and had a history of abuse. Her grandmother was raising her and was concerned about the young woman's recent pattern of poor decisions. I met with the young girl for about fifty minutes and we talked about her history, what she wanted to discuss in treatment, and how counseling could help. She was the only client I had that evening. I went home and couldn't sleep. All night I tossed and turned, thinking what I could do to help this girl. I worried about her making more bad decisions. I wondered what I needed to do in order to prevent her from damaging her life even further. After what seemed like days, I got up the next morning and went to school. I was physically and emotionally exhausted. I remember thinking there was no way I could do that every night. I only had one client! What about when I had dozens? Surely, I could not survive in this career if I continued in such a way.

It took several years, but I finally figured out how to manage this. For the first part of my career I judged my effectiveness by how my clients performed. If they got better and showed improvement, then that meant I was a good psychologist. The opposite applied as well; if they didn't improve then I was a poor psychologist. I ultimately realized this was both untrue and unfair. How could I judge my performance based on the efforts of someone else? I needed to judge my performance based on the merits of the performance itself. If I gave good counsel, was a good listener, and provided appropriate insights, then for that day I was a good psychologist. It didn't matter whether the client went home and applied anything I said; that was their decision and completely outside of my control. However, if I was derelict in my responsibilities and did not provide quality professional help, then for that day I was a poor psychologist. To this day I hold this philosophy. Every day I try to do my best to help clients. Whether they change is not for me to manage. I cannot control it and therefore do my best not to worry about it.

Jacob understood this principle. He believed his job was to preach the gospel as best he could. If he did that, he was successful and worthy of approbation. If he did not preach the gospel to the best of his abilities, then he felt like he was responsible for the collateral damage of sin that his followers might experience. By being responsible for something he could control, which was preaching the gospel, he was able to narrow his focus and not feel overwhelmed. Trying to control something you cannot control is a great way to increase your anxiety. Instead, identify those areas in your life where you actually have control. Focus your efforts on those areas. *Do not* spend your energy in areas where you do not have control. It is quite simple to create these distinctions. As a starting point, use the following rule of thumb. If it relates to you and your personal choices, you have control. If it relates to *anyone else*, including children, spouses, students, clients, patients, customers, *you do not have control.* You cannot manipulate outcomes in others. Take control of *your* behavior and choices and leave the rest to the Lord.

Principle #2: Do difficult things

"But, notwithstanding the greatness of the task, I must do according to the strict commands of God, and tell you concerning your wickedness and abominations, in the presence of the pure in heart, and the broken heart, and under the glance of the piercing eye of the Almighty God." (Jacob 2:10)

This scripture comes at the beginning of one of Jacob's sermons to the Nephites. The people had two main problems at the time: one small and one big. The smaller problem had to do with their seeking riches and becoming selfish and prideful. Jacob didn't seem so worried about talking with them about that. The larger problem had to do with the Nephite men. They had become lecherous and were violating covenants of chastity by seeking out prostitutes. It seems Jacob did not relish the idea of addressing such a sensitive topic but felt compelled to do so by the Spirit (see Jacob 2:22-23). He acknowledged the task was potentially overwhelming but knew it was what he needed to do. Having been commanded of God to communicate His will to the people, it was essential Jacob followed through regardless of his personal fears or hesitancies.

Anxiety thrives on fear of the unknown. We get worked up over the things we know we need to do, but we are afraid to move forward. We create all sorts of fictions in our minds about how terrible the outcome may be if we proceed. Paralyzed with indecision, we remain stuck for days, months, years and even decades. The more we avoid the fearful task, the greater our anxiety becomes. I have seen this play out time and time again in the lives of my friends and associates. There is one simple way to defeat this pattern. We must engage in the act that brings us so much fear. In almost every case, our degree of fear associated with the potential outcome is unfounded. In fact, when people actually do the thing they are afraid of, they almost always say, "That wasn't as bad as I thought." They didn't like doing it and aren't getting right back in line to do it again, but it *wasn't as bad as they thought.* Those sorts of experiences are critical in anxiety management. Anxiety reduction will never occur if we perpetually avoid those things that make us anxious. Jacob knew the task. It was scary and part of him did not want to do it. He did it anyway. As we strive to do those things that are difficult, we will find our capacities will increase and our anxieties will decrease.

Principle #3: Accept your weakness

"Wherefore, we search the prophets, and we have many revelations and the spirit of prophecy; and having all these witnesses we obtain a hope, and our faith becometh unshaken, insomuch that we truly can command in the name of Jesus and the very trees obey us, or the mountains, or the waves of the sea. Nevertheless, the Lord God showeth us our weakness that we may know that it is by his grace, and his great condescensions unto the children of men, that we have power to do these things." (Jacob 4:6-7)

Jacob begins this scripture by referring to pretty awesome power: trees, mountains and waves of the sea being subjected to his will! He cites "unshaken faith" as the source of this ability. Yet in the very next statement he refers to the true source of his power: our Father in Heaven. He further teaches how the Lord kept him humble despite such power when he says, "The Lord God *showeth us our weakness.*" As God showed Jacob's weakness to him, it allowed him to keep things in perspective and fully acknowledge his personal limitations while still enjoying greatly enhanced capacities.

Anxiety is a very common human frailty. Everyone experiences it to one degree or another. Millions worldwide suffer to the point of partial incapacitation. Why would our loving Father in Heaven permit such a scourge to afflict His children? There are many answers to the question, not the least of which being because He knows we need to remain humble and trust in Him. As Mormon reviewed the voluminous records to abridge Nephite history, he saw the cycle of prosperity, pride and destruction happen over and over again. In a parenthetical comment he concludes the following:

> Yea, and we may see at the very time when he doth prosper his people, yea, in the increase of their fields, their flocks and their herds, and in gold, and in silver, and in all manner of precious things of every kind and art; sparing their lives, and delivering them out of the hands of their enemies; softening the hearts of their enemies that they should not declare wars against them; yea, and in fine, doing all things for the welfare and happiness of his people; yea, then is the time that they do harden their hearts, and do forget the Lord their God, and do trample under their feet the Holy One—yea, and this because of their ease, and their exceedingly great prosperity. And thus we see that except the Lord doth chasten his people with many afflictions, yea, except he doth visit them with death and with terror, and with famine and with

all manner of pestilence, they will not remember him. (Helaman 12:2-3)

This pattern has not changed much since Nephite times. We continue to reap the blessings so generously given by God and then promptly forget their source. It reminds me of the anecdote of a man who falls down a steep embankment towards a cliff. He cries out in prayer, "Lord, help me!" Out of nowhere he sees a large branch that he grabs hold to stop his fall. He then says, "Never mind, Lord; I was able to take care of it myself." Perhaps anxiety is one of those ways in which the Lord "chastens his people with many afflictions." I've worked with many people who have anxiety. What's even worse, *they have anxiety about having anxiety*. They think something has gone terribly wrong because they have this dread condition that causes them grief. I'm suggesting we try to see our afflictions in a different light. We may have less overall turmoil if we view our weakness as a condition that keeps us humble and provides opportunities for growth. In the case of anxiety, following this practice will not cure our fears. However, it will prevent us from heaping additional panic on top of an already existing anxiety condition. Worrying about being worried is overkill. If we can accept the fact that we are flawed and weak, we will have one less thing to worry about. We still have the uphill battle of conquering our fears, but we can do it with our burden lightened.

Principle #4: Don't reject counsel

"Wherefore, brethren, seek not to counsel the Lord, but to take counsel from his hand. For behold, ye yourselves know that he counseleth in wisdom, and in justice, and in great mercy, over all his works." (Jacob 4:10)

Previously, we discussed the concept of agency. It is a wonderful gift that is crucial to our spiritual development. As with any blessing from the Lord, Satan seeks to compromise or corrupt it. One of his strategies with agency is to have us believe we know best and do not need to rely on the advice or counsel of others. Consider the story of Naaman from the Old Testament (see 2 Kings 5). He was commander of the armies of Syria. This was an extremely powerful and prestigious position. His commands to soldiers were likely followed without question. I imagine many sought his counsel regarding important matters. At one point in his life he discovered he had contracted leprosy. Leprosy is a terrible disease that can cause permanent damage to the body, even death in some cases. This condition would have been of great concern to Naaman, probably forecasting the premature end of his military career.

Having heard of a prophet in Israel who could do miracles, Naaman inquired after him. He arrived at the home of Elisha the prophet in grand style, complete with servants, horses and chariot. He went to the door and waited. Elisha did not come to the door. Instead, one of the servants answered the door with a message from his master. The message was this: go and bathe in the river Jordan seven times, and you will be clean from your disease. Without additional fanfare, the servant retreated and Naaman was left standing on the prophet's doorstep. Naaman was furious! How dare Elisha not come out himself! Did he not know of the fame and position of Naaman? Naaman was accustomed to commanding and getting his way. Yet after making a long journey, this prophet did not have the courtesy to even meet him in person. Naaman had evidently expected Elisha to come and perform some grand miracle, curing his leprosy on the spot. Such was not the case. He was left there to fume over the recent turn of events.

In addition to feeling slighted by the prophet, Naaman was even more upset by what he considered to be ridiculous counsel. Wash in the Jordan River seven times? Was this a joke? Naaman ranted that there were much better rivers in his country; why should he go to the dirty Jordan and be played a fool? Since when did washing in river water cure leprosy? It appeared Naaman's trip to Israel had been wasted, and he left the place in fierce anger. Fortunately, he had thoughtful servants who were brave enough to approach their master with additional advice. "And his servants came near, and spake unto him, and said, My father, if the prophet had bid thee do some great thing, wouldest thou not have done it? how much rather then, when he saith to thee, Wash, and be clean?" (2 Kings 5:13). What wonderful counsel! Even today there are some who say they'd be willing to sacrifice everything to travel by handcart to build the New Jerusalem, but in the same breath reject a calling to serve in the Primary. All heavenly counsel is an opportunity for growth, whether the counsel be great or small. To his credit, Naaman agreed with his servants. He went to the River Jordan and entered. After the first immersion, I imagine he came out wet and muddy, while still leprous. He went down another time, and another with the same result. After four or five times I can almost hear Lucifer whispering in his ear: "Are you stupid or something? How foolish you look to your servants! Here you are, the captain of the Syrian guard, and you are dunking yourself over and over in a muddy river. Thousands stand at your command and yet you just took advice from the servant of an alleged prophet you have never met. Quit making yourself look like an idiot and get out of the river before it ruins your reputation completely."

I'm sure the temptation was strong to quit and go back to Syria. Yet there was something in Naaman that made him continue. With each successive immersion bringing compounded disappointment, the seventh brought the prophesied healing. He came forth from the water that time clean and whole. Humble and grateful, Naaman returned to the house of Elisha, this time being able to speak with the prophet directly. He expressed his gratitude and offered payment for the heavenly service. Elisha, being a dutiful servant of God, refused the payment and credited heaven for the miracle.

Those who struggle with anxiety rightly pray for relief. Seeking heavenly help for all of our problems is appropriate and good. The problem comes when we don't follow the divine counsel received or don't recognize it as such. Sometimes we expect, as Naaman, for some grand and miraculous event to occur to heal us from our afflictions. Yet in almost every case, miracles are more subtle. Say you have been praying for ways to manage anxiety. What you might hope is that the next day you'll hear of a new miracle drug that will cure all anxiety, all the time, with no side effects, at a very affordable price. That would truly be a miracle! It would be just like the miracle Naaman expected; Elisha would have come out of his home in impressive fashion and called upon the powers of heaven. Thunder would roll, lightning would strike, and angels would sing as Naaman's skin became clean. But no such miracle occurred for Naaman. Such miracles are similarly unlikely today. So, instead of the miracle drug announcement, you get a phone call from a bishopric counselor inviting you to speak in sacrament meeting. "Is he crazy? Doesn't he know I have anxiety? I can't speak in public!" Can you hear the echoes of Naaman's rant as well? "Is Elisha crazy? Doesn't he know river water can't cure leprosy?"

Like Naaman, Jacob understood the need to follow the Lord's direction, regardless of how misdirected or ineffective it might seem in his own mortal perspective. I testify that not only does our Father in Heaven love us tremendously, He knows everything. His counsel is always perfect. If He can make rivers cure leprosy, then He can make assignments to speak in sacrament meeting alleviate anxiety. Always ask for the Lord's help, but take extra care to ensure you are willing to follow His direction, no matter what. Don't rationalize your way out of a possible miracle because you don't understand everything just yet.

Principle #5: Maintain spiritual nourishment

"Wherefore, my beloved brethren, I beseech of you in words of soberness that ye would repent, and come with full purpose of heart, and cleave unto God as he cleaveth unto you. And while his arm of mercy is extended towards you in the light of the day, harden not your hearts." (Jacob 6:5)

Too many people believe change is outside of their grasp. This becomes particularly salient with individuals who have struggled with the same issues for many years. Those who have tried diligently but unsuccessfully to change can become very discouraged. They start to believe they will always be stuck with their problems. This mindset is not inspired of God but is a tool of the adversary. We can always change as long as we desire to do so *and* reach out for heavenly help. Elder Terrance M. Vinson of the Seventy told the following story:

> A young boy was trying to smooth out the dirt area behind his house so he could play there with his cars. There was a large rock obstructing his work. The boy pushed and pulled with all his might, but no matter how hard he tried, the rock wouldn't budge. His father watched for a while, then came to his son and said, "You need to use all your strength to move a rock this large." The boy responded, "I have used all my strength!" His father corrected him: "No you haven't. You haven't had my help yet!" They then

bent down together and moved the rock easily. [5]

Jacob's counsel is to "cleave unto God." This suggests more than just a casual or relaxed relationship. Cleave means to hold fast to, or to cling to very strongly. Becoming casual in our relationship with Father in Heaven will create distance between us and Him. It will decrease our reliance on the Spirit and increase the influence of the world in our lives. This distance will also decrease our overall spiritual sensitivity. This can be a particularly dangerous condition, as the longer we go without spiritual nourishment, the less we recognize our need for it. Consider physical hunger. When we are hungry, our bodies constantly remind us. As the body needs nourishment, it will start to call louder and louder for something to eat. You'll recognize these calls. They are quite common at the last hour of your fast on fast Sunday, when you smell the roast but know you shouldn't eat for another sixty minutes. Such hunger pangs can be intense. We feel a strong desire to eat as soon as we can. The longer we go without food, the more intense the cravings become.

Spiritual hunger is different. Our spirits need daily nourishment, just as our bodies do. However, as we stop feeding our spirits, we stop recognizing spiritual hunger cues. The effect can be catastrophic to our spiritual development. Even though we may be spiritually starving, we have no indicators that drive us to seek spiritual food. Individuals can go years without feeding their spirits and yet have no idea their spiritual condition is so desperate. Ironically, it is when we are close to the Spirit and feasting regularly that we realize we need ongoing nourishment. The person who reads her scriptures daily and then misses a day may notice a dip in her spirituality and a prompting to get back on track. But the person who has not read his scriptures for a decade will not likely have any such prompting and will go on in the ways of spiritual starvation.

Hardening our hearts and refusing spiritual nourishment will decrease our ability to feel the Spirit. I believe this will increase feelings of anxiety as well. The Spirit is known as the Comforter, while the adversary is the "father of contention" (3 Nephi 11:29). The influence

5 Terrance M. Vinson, "Drawing Closer to God," *Ensign*, November 2013, 105.

of the Spirit brings peace and contentment. It helps us relax and be confident in uncertain times. As we distance ourselves from that influence, we are likely to experience greater emotional distress. I'm not suggesting anxiety is exclusively a product of spiritual darkness. I'm simply suggesting regardless of the source of our fears and worries, the influence of the Spirit can mitigate such feelings. Jacob's life and example provide strong evidence that spiritual truths can help resolve mental health issues.

Practical suggestions for change:

Follow the five outlined principles from the life of Jacob:

1. be appropriately accountable
2. do difficult things
3. accept your weakness
4. don't reject counsel
5. maintain spiritual nourishment

Understand that our minds and spirits are connected, so that spiritual remedies can have influence on emotional challenges.

CHAPTER FIVE
Using Greater Mindfulness to Manage Thoughts and Emotions

"But your mind has been on the things of the earth more than on the things of me, your Maker, and the ministry whereunto you have been called." (D&C 30:2)

Often when I suggest to clients they have the power to modify their feelings, I'm met with resistance. They say they've tried to change and always failed. Initially I assumed clients weren't trying hard enough—the methods and strategies we discussed in counseling were true and helpful. However, even when clients were fully motivated to change, and had applied the tools, they weren't always seeing progress. What was the problem?

I realized a scenario where even the combination of full client motivation and helpful tools for change could still result in repeated failure to change. Let's imagine you are driving a car down a road. At the end of this road is a one-thousand-foot sheer cliff. There is no barrier at the end of the road. You are about one mile from the edge and are traveling eighty miles an hour. You continue to accelerate as you drive toward the precipice. About one hundred feet before the edge of the cliff, you see a large sign that says, "Danger! Cliff 100 feet ahead!" You slam on the brakes with all the force you can produce. Unfortunately, the laws of physics take over and your car goes over the cliff.

As we examine this situation, we find the following elements. The car functions properly and the brakes work just fine. Brakes stop cars, and the brakes on your car were perfectly capable of stopping you. We can't blame the brakes in this case; they were suitable for the intended purpose of stopping. How about your motivation? Well, you had plenty of motivation to stop. You pressed on the brake pedal just as hard as you could. We can't blame your motivation in this case; you did exactly what you should do to stop a car from going off a cliff. Then, what was the problem? Why did the combination of motivation and proper strategies not work to achieve the desired goal?

I think we all know what the problem was. You can't stop a speeding car from going over a cliff if the first time you hit the brakes is one hundred feet before the edge. In fact, it would only take about one second for the car to travel that remaining one hundred feet, even with you hitting the brakes. No car is going to come to a stop in one second at such dramatic speeds. *The problem was not hitting the brakes soon enough.* Brakes work; motivation works; but there needs to be a sufficient amount of time to employ the correct solution in order for it to be effective. If the same person was traveling one hundred miles per hour but hit the brakes one mile before the edge of the cliff, there would be no problem in safely stopping the car long before the precipice was reached.

I was wrong to judge those who I thought "weren't trying hard enough." I believed they had low motivation for change, but I was wrong. Their motivation was strong, but their timing was off. The mechanism for change worked as well but was being applied too late. I have met with many, many people who attempt to manage their anxiety the same way the driver attempted to stop the car in the scenario. Their anxiety symptoms have them traveling at one hundred miles per hour. At the last minute before an emotional cliff, they try to apply some of the anxiety management strategies they have learned. Although the strategies work, they work about as well as brakes applied with insufficient time to stop. These clients go off the emotional cliff time and time again. They come back to me and say, "The anxiety techniques don't work; I've tried them over and over and they don't change the way I feel." Yet a more careful analysis of the situation suggests the problem lies with the *timing* of the intervention, and not with the intervention itself. It's critical to help clients understand the difference as they work towards anxiety reduction. "Brakes don't work to stop cars from going over cliffs" is inaccurate, when the true problem is not applying brakes soon enough. By the same token, "Anxiety reduction strategies don't work to reduce anxiety" is similarly inaccurate, when the true problem is not applying such strategies early enough.

So, what can be done to apply anxiety reduction strategies sooner than later? First, be more mindful of the situation. In the previous example, there was a warning sign. It warned the driver the cliff was coming, but the sign was only one hundred feet before the edge of the cliff. While this is partially helpful, it certainly does not give the driver enough time to stop if the car is already speeding. What if there were multiple warning signs? I remember going on a family vacation years ago. We were driving on a winding road that also had a fairly steep decline. We passed a sign that said, "Runaway truck ramp: three miles ahead." For those who are unaware, runaway truck ramps are common on major roads with steep downgrades. It is a steep incline, usually many hundred feet in length, designed to help an out-of-control truck stop quickly and safely.

After the first sign, there were many other signs that followed: "Runaway truck ramp: two and half miles ahead; runaway truck ramp: two miles ahead; runaway truck ramp: one and a half miles ahead." There were so many signs that at one point it became a little comical. I felt like I was watching a series of teaser trailers for a well-anticipated movie. More signs appeared, each one announcing a smaller distance. At last, the time arrived. We pulled around a corner and a large sign with a prominent arrow announced we were there! "RUNAWAY TRUCK RAMP" was just to the right, a steep incline with deep sand. Fortunately, we were not in a runaway truck and had no need for the ramp, so we continued on our journey. I reflected on the warning signs. Why did there have to be so many? There were probably no fewer than ten signs bringing attention to the upcoming ramp. As I thought about the situation, it became clear. If I were caught in a truck that was careening out of control and picking up speed by the minute, I would want to know there was help arriving soon. I would want to be prepared to pull off the road and try to enter the ramp safely. The more time I had to plan my approach the better chance I'd have to keep myself and others from harm. Even if, in my stress and panic, I missed seeing one of the warning signs, surely I would see one of the many others. If there were only a single sign showing the way to the ramp I might miss it or be otherwise unprepared to make a safe exit.

When dealing with anxiety symptoms, what if we had similar warning signs? Imagine if we had signs that said, "MAJOR ANXIETY ISSUES; THREE HOURS AHEAD" or "PANIC ATTACK; TWO HOURS AHEAD." That's much better than the typical warning that most people describe. Many indicate they seem to have no idea when serious anxiety symptoms will strike. Either they get no warning, or they have some sort of sign that says, "PANIC ATTACK; TEN SECONDS AHEAD." There's not much one can do about a significant panic attack with only ten seconds notice. Although preventing the panic attack is the primary goal, sometimes just *surviving it* seems like a goal in and of itself. Many have described panic attacks as feeling like heart attacks. They'll often go to the emergency room only to be told there is nothing wrong with their heart, but they've had a panic attack. There are many symptoms of panic attacks. Some of the more common ones include heart palpitations, dizziness, tightness in the chest, breathing difficulty, and feeling a loss of control. Symptoms often appear suddenly and typically last anywhere between three and ten minutes. In almost every case a panic attack will resolve of its own volition. However, that three to ten minutes can be extremely frightening and seem like an eternity. What can one do to better manage symptoms during a panic attack? Here are some suggestions:

Try to slow your breathing. In contrast to the shallow, rapid breathing often associated with panic attacks, try to intentionally take deep breaths. Control the inhale and the exhale. Breathe in through your nose and out through your mouth with deep breaths, over and over, until the anxiety subsides.

Realize you are having a panic attack and what that means. Like we reviewed before, people often mistake a panic attack for a heart attack. Heart attacks have different symptoms. If you are prone to panic attacks you are familiar with how they feel. You may have even had a doctor tell you your heart is fine, and it is anxiety you experience. People who have panic attacks often believe they are going to die. If you recognize you are not going to die and that the attack will resolve itself in a matter of minutes, that can help you avoid adding death anxiety to the already strong anxiety of the panic attack.

Try to reduce external input. Your senses process all the information around them. When having a panic attack, try to reduce the amount of information your senses have to process. If you can, close your eyes. Try to get to a place where it is quiet. Let your body focus on less input while you are trying to deal with the emergency of the moment.

Attempt to redirect your thoughts to something simple and peaceful. As you try to distract your mind from the anxiety you can deal with the panic attack more effectively. Some people have a "happy place" they have been to or would like to go to. They try to imagine this calm and peaceful place. For me, I love to think of the beach, with a gentle breeze and the slow, rhythmic sound of the waves. Thinking of a peaceful situation can create greater calm.

Repeat a calming, reassuring phrase. Panic attacks often involve many inaccurate and extreme thoughts such as "I'm going to die" or "I'm going to lose my mind." These are false and only serve to fuel the anxiety. Try to replace such thoughts with simple, accurate thoughts that promote peace. This could be something like "I'll get through this" or "peace, be still." You should choose your own phrase; something that makes sense and has personal meaning to you. Repeat that phrase over and over, slowly, while you endure the panic attack.

Successfully enduring a panic attack is a short-term strategy. Long-term anxiety management requires greater awareness of the circumstances that contribute to feelings of anxiety in general. This is similar to learning to recognize warning signs in our own lives, like the runaway truck ramp signs in the former example. Besides panic attacks, there are other types of anxiety that tend to be long-term. They don't have strong peaks like panic attacks but have ongoing feelings of stress or worry. They can include social anxiety, generalized anxiety, and other types. The panic attack management symptoms previously discussed can work for these situations as well but not as effectively. One of the keys to learning more effective anxiety management is to become aware of the situations that tend to precede both acute and chronic anxiety symptoms. Some of these situations will be external, but many of them are internal. Becoming more aware of our own thoughts and feelings is critical in learning how to better manage anxiety and helping to stop it before it gets out of control.

Lehi, the exiled prophet from Jerusalem, had a remarkable vision of the tree of life. He described the vision to his family. While some were unimpressed, his son Nephi was very moved. In fact, Nephi wanted to see the vision for himself. After earnest prayer and meditation, his desire was granted. He saw all the things his father saw, including many other things that were crucial for the future of his civilization. At one point his doubting brothers, Laman and Lemuel, complained they were not able to understand the symbolism of their father's dream. Nephi graciously explained to them what they could have discovered for themselves had they applied the same time and effort Nephi did. His brothers asked the question, "What meaneth the river of water which our father saw?" (1 Nephi 15:26). Nephi answered, "The water which my father saw was filthiness; *and so much was his mind swallowed up in other things that he beheld not the filthiness of the water*" (1 Nephi 15:27, emphasis added). Lehi's original description of the water did not include that it was dirty; only that it ran next to the tree of life. It appears Lehi missed this detail because as Nephi described, "His mind was swallowed up in other things." These "other things" were likely important, no doubt, but even so they obscured Lehi's vision in the moment.

How often do our minds get "swallowed up in other things" that we do not pay sufficient attention to the subtle cues of our emotions or experiences? Recently I had an experience that taught me an important lesson about this. I determined I was not feeling the Spirit as much as I should on a daily basis. There were times when I made poor decisions that impacted my relationships. I remember thinking the Holy Ghost could warn me against such decisions, thus giving me the opportunity to choose more wisely before the fact. I was driving home and praying out loud, asking Father in Heaven to essentially "increase the volume" of my spiritual promptings. I reasoned that if I more clearly heard the prompting, I'd be better able to follow it. In response to my plea, I received a distinct and stunning answer. As I asked for stronger spiritual impressions that I could understand more distinctly, the Spirit said, "I need you to listen more carefully." I felt humbled and chastened. As usual, the Spirit was exactly correct. I was not taking appropriate accountability. I had the "worldly volume" in my life turned up, and I was asking the Spirit to shout over the blare of the terrestrial din. The Spirit told me to turn down the worldly volume and listen more intently to the still, small voice. Recall the experience of Elijah as he was asked to present himself before the Lord: "And, behold, the Lord passed by, and a great and strong wind rent the mountains, and brake in pieces the rocks before the Lord; but the Lord was not in the wind: and after the wind an earthquake; but the Lord was not in the earthquake: And after the earthquake a fire; but the Lord was not in the fire: and after the fire a still small voice" (1 Kings 19:11-12). I was asking for wind and earthquake and fire to grab my attention; the Lord asked me to quiet my mind and listen more intently to the still, small voice. It was a wonderful lesson.

An important part of anxiety management is learning to quiet our minds and become more aware of our experiences, both spiritual and temporal. All anxiety experiences have a precursor. Learning to recognize what comes before anxiety gives us a better chance to intervene with sufficient time and stop the feelings before they become unmanageable. One such strategy to accomplish this is meditation.

Meditation is the process of increasing one's awareness of their own thoughts and internal experiences. Enhanced mindfulness can be a product of effective meditation. Consider an example of how this could relate to a common anxiety reaction. Imagine you walk into a grocery store and it is much more crowded than you anticipated. You had planned your trip so that there would likely be only a few other customers, but for whatever reason that is not the case. You start to have the familiar anxious experience you get when in large groups of people: increased heart rate, sweaty palms, feeling flushed, and a strong desire to immediately leave. If you have no further awareness of your anxiety except for the physical experience, the anxiety intensity will likely increase unhindered. Now consider the same scenario but with an expanded thought process. You enter the store, there are more people than you thought would be there, and feelings of anxiety start to increase. You have the following thoughts: "Right now I'm feeling anxiety because there are more people here than I previously thought. I tend to feel more anxious when things go contrary to my plans. I don't like being around others because I fear they are going to judge me in their minds. I worry about what they are probably thinking about me and this makes me feel nervous. It makes me feel like I want to leave so I don't have to think about all of the things that are wrong with me."

In both situations the anxiety reaction is the same; the feelings are intense, and the fear is real. However, in the second situation, the person has greater insight into what is likely causing the anxiety. With such insight, there is more that can be done. Inaccurate thoughts can be challenged. Sometimes, simply being aware of what is causing a situation can bring a little relief, even though the situation hasn't changed. Have you ever been in heavy traffic and had no idea why it is happening? I've been there, and it can be quite frustrating. *How long is the traffic going to last? What is going on?* Then I find out there is an accident one mile ahead, and after the accident the traffic will increase to normal speeds. Even though I'm still stuck in the same traffic I was thirty seconds ago, I have a little more peace knowing 1) what is actually happening and 2) that it will likely resolve soon. Anxiety is fueled by fear of the unknown. As we increase awareness of what causes anxiety, how it is manifest, and what can be done to decrease the symptoms, overall anxiety will decrease. As I mentioned before, some people have anxiety *about having anxiety.* That can become overwhelming in very short order. Increasing personal awareness will decrease anxiety and bring greater self-control.

Meditation takes practice and discipline. Essentially, meditation is a way of forcing your mind to take a needed break. We are all familiar with the concept of physical rest. None of us believe we could push our physical bodies 24/7, without any reprieve, and not experience consequences. In fact, the body has its own means of taking care of itself if it is pushed too far without sufficient rest. People have been known to simply collapse from exhaustion, whether they wanted to or not. Their bodies needed rest, so their bodies eventually took control and got the rest they needed. I believe the mind works the same way, yet we don't understand this nearly as much. If you believe you can run your mind at full power, 24/7, without any sort of break, and still experience full mental effectiveness, you are incorrect. Your mind will do the same as your body when it gets tired; performance will decrease and eventually slow to the point of being ineffective. Mental rest does not happen automatically; it usually needs to be intentional. When you sleep your body gets physical rest. Does your mind also rest when you sleep? Not necessarily. Have you ever had a dream that feels very real, complete with emotions? Some experience nightmares that are vivid and evoke a strong sense of fear and anxiety. Although their bodies are at rest during such experiences, their minds are overloaded and overwhelmed. If you want to achieve mental rest, you need to do this intentionally.

One of the spiritual benefits of meditation is greater personal peace. The Savior was an excellent example of taking time to commune and spiritually prepare. Prior to the formal start of his mortal ministry, He fasted for forty days and forty nights. He took time to focus his thoughts. Mark recorded the following event in the Savior's life: "And in the morning, rising up a great while before day, he [Jesus] went out, and departed into a solitary place, and there prayed" (Mark 1:35). He got up early, went to a separate place, and took time to pray to His father. This is an excellent pattern. If Mark were recording the story of my life, I'm afraid he might say something like, "In the morning, after hitting the snooze button a few times, he rolled out of bed and only had time for a quick prayer because he was going to be late for work." Perhaps you can relate. We follow the example of the Savior by being intentional, creating sufficient time and circumstances to effectively commune with our Father in Heaven.

Another spiritual benefit of meditation is increased revelation. Nephi wanted to experience the vision of the tree of life that his father Lehi had experienced. Nephi recounts his preparation for this event as follows: "For it came to pass after I had desired to know the things that my father had seen, and believing that the Lord was able to make them known unto me, *as I sat pondering in mine heart* I was caught away in the Spirit of the Lord, yea, into an exceedingly high mountain, which I never had before seen, and upon which I never had before set my foot" (1 Nephi 11:1, emphasis added). The revelation came only after he desired to know, believed he could receive, and took the time to clear his mind and think carefully on the things of the Spirit. As another example, the latter-day prophet Joseph F. Smith wanted greater information regarding what happens in the spirit world. He only had a few scriptures that shed light on this topic but none of them contained great detail. President Smith had read these scriptures and wanted to know more. He recorded the following: "*As I pondered over these things which are written*, the eyes of my understanding were opened, and the Spirit of the Lord rested upon me, and I saw the hosts of the dead, both small and great" (D&C 138:11, emphasis added). Pondering, which is a suitable synonym for meditation, can lead to great personal insights.

If we are too busy, or have too much on our minds, we can miss opportunities to receive revelation or achieve greater personal peace. President Harold B. Lee related the following story, as he received it from President David O. McKay:

> The Twelve will not soon forget President David O. McKay's admonition in our council meeting one morning when he impressed the vital importance of taking time to meditate in order to keep spiritually attuned. ... "It's a great thing to be responsive to the whisperings of the Spirit and we know that when these whisperings come it is a gift and our privilege to have them. They come when we are relaxed and not under pressure of appointments." The President then took occasion to relate an experience in the life of Bishop John Wells, formerly a member of the Presiding Bishopric. A son of Bishop Wells was killed in Emigration Canyon on a railroad track. ... His boy was run over by a freight train. Sister Wells was inconsolable. She mourned during the three days prior to the funeral, received no comfort at the funeral, and was in a rather serious state of mind. One day soon after the funeral services, while she was lying on her bed relaxed, still mourning, she claims that her son appeared to her and said, "Mother, do not mourn. Do not cry. I am all right." He told her that she did not understand how the accident happened. He explained that he had given a signal to the engineer to move on and then made the usual effort to catch the railings on the freight train, but as he attempted to do so his foot caught in a root and he failed to catch the hand rail and his body fell under the train. It was clearly an accident. He said that as soon as he realized that he was in another environment he tried to see his father but he could not reach him. His father was so busy with the duties in the office that he could not respond to his call; therefore, he had come to his mother and

he said to her, "You tell Father that all is well with me. I want you to not mourn anymore." [6]

Do we ever find ourselves so "busy with the duties of the office" or with duties of the home, the social media, the video game, even the church calling, that we are unable to effectively tune in to things of the Spirit? If so, we need to take opportunity to center our minds and thoughts, allowing sufficient time to achieve a measure of personal peace even if only for a few minutes.

Regarding meditation, President David O. McKay also stated, "We pay too little attention to the value of meditation, a principle of devotion. In our worship there are two elements: One is spiritual communion arising from our own meditation; the other, instruction from others, particularly from those who have authority to guide and instruct us. Of the two, the more profitable introspectively is the meditation. Meditation is the language of the soul.... Meditation is a form of prayer.... Meditation is one of the most secret, most sacred doors through which we pass into the presence of the Lord." [7]

As noted previously, developing the skill of meditation to become mindful takes practice and discipline. Many in today's society are constantly overwhelmed by thoughts including mental to-do lists, regrets about the past, and worries about the future. The idea of taking a "mental break" seems almost impossible. *It is* possible to take such a break, but it needs to be intentional. There are many different types of meditation. The following suggestions are examples that include a spiritual focus as well. Here are some practical steps you can use in order to create a habit of effective meditation.

Find a quiet time and space, free from distraction. I know this can be nearly impossible in some situations, but do your best. Effective meditation needs to be free from distraction. Some may choose the early morning, others may prefer later in the evening. Try to choose a time and place where you will not be interrupted. Make sure you will have

---

6 Harold B. Lee, *Teachings of Presidents of the Church: Harold B. Lee* (Salt Lake City: The Church of Jesus Christ of Latter-day Saints, 2000) 182-183.

7 David O. McKay, *Teachings of Presidents of the Church: David O. McKay* (Salt Lake City: The Church of Jesus Christ of Latter-day Saints, 2003) 31-32.

sufficient time, so that you don't feel pressured to rush through the experience. Try to choose a time when you are not overly tired. Meditation will not be effective if you are physically exhausted. At first, don't worry about frequency, but try to be consistent. If you are only able to find a quiet time and space once per week, then start with that. If you can find such a time more frequently, that's fine as well. Remember, *this time and experience is for your benefit.* Try not to burden yourself with thoughts of "I'm doing it wrong" or "I'm not doing it frequently enough."

Begin with prayer. Take time to kneel in prayer and talk with your Father in Heaven. Tell Him about your day and what you are feeling. Thank Him for the many, many blessings you have received. Let Him know you are attempting to have a brief time of meditation and ask Him for help. Ask Him to help you focus and relax, trying to achieve the goal you have set out to do. Try not to be hasty or rushed in your prayer; take as much time as you can and let the Holy Ghost enter into your heart.

Study the scriptures. Prior to your meditation, even earlier in the day, give some thought to scriptures that you could read that will help you focus your thoughts and achieve calm. You may have a favorite group of scriptures that helps you feel peace. After praying, take time to carefully read these verses. Don't read too quickly. Take your time, reflecting upon every sentence. Think about the placement of words and the context of the verses. Stop periodically and think about what you just read. Think about how it applies to you in your life. Go back and read verses over and over if necessary. You don't need to get through a large volume of scripture during this time. In some cases, you may read the same verse over and over, pondering and reflecting on its meaning. Make sure you spend adequate time in this step. Sometimes we view scripture study as "one more thing" we need to do in order to complete our daily spiritual checklist. Resist that feeling as you study the word of God in this setting. Allow sufficient time to really reflect upon what the scriptures mean and what the Lord is trying to teach you.

As you begin the actual meditation, do your best to follow these steps:

Find a comfortable sitting position. Be aware of your body sensations. How does the environment feel around you? Close your eyes and try to minimize input from the external world. You will notice things like how your body feels, what your mind is thinking, and even the strangeness of the experience if it is new to you. Allow yourself to have these experiences but try not to dwell on them; acknowledge them and let them pass.

Focus on your breathing. This can be a very effective method to achieve greater mindfulness. Slow your breathing down so that you are taking slow, measured breaths. It should feel natural yet deliberate. Let your mind focus on the rhythm of your breathing, as your chest expands and contracts.

Notice your thoughts. At first, you will have many thoughts that pass through your mind. All of them can serve as potential distractors. Do your best to not be preoccupied by them. Simply acknowledge them and let them pass by. Think of this process as if you were sitting by a gently flowing river. As you sit there, you see various things floating past you. There is a leaf, then a branch, then another leaf, etc. You are sitting calmly on the river's edge, watching these things pass by. You don't jump in the river to get them, or poke them with a stick, or run along the bank to follow them. You simply see them, notice them, and then let them pass along their way. Try to do this with your thoughts. When a thought arises such as, "You've got to pick up the kids in 20 minutes," acknowledge it, and let it pass on through your mind. Try to avoid thinking about how you'll need to pick them up, grab dinner afterwards, get gas in the car, and then help them with homework. Those are all good things and will happen in due time, but in your meditation moment, let those plans go for a minute. Allow your thoughts to pass through your mind without focusing on them. There will be time for that later, but not during the meditation experience.

Conclude intentionally. We are all busy and likely don't have unlimited time for meditation breaks. Even if we did, that's not the point. Meditation should be conscious, planned, and a distinct break from daily routine. We meditate and then we get back to the regular pace of life. Some may have plenty of uninterrupted time and can meditate for as long as they want in the moment, concluding when they feel they are complete. If you are busy and find it difficult to take the time to meditate, be intentional about how much time you will spend. If it is only five to ten minutes, then take that full time to engage in the process. When you are done with your appointed time, take a minute to reflect on the event.

End with prayer. After you are done with your meditation, take another opportunity to kneel and thank your Father in Heaven for the experience you had. Ask Him for help to improve the experience next time. Pray that this ongoing practice will allow you to achieve greater peace and less worry in your daily experience.

Developing a practice of meditation takes time and effort but can yield great emotional and spiritual results. If you make this a priority in your life and seek Heaven's help to have the time and space to do it, you will find eventual success over.

Practical suggestions for change:

Begin a practice of regular meditation following the outlined principles.

Develop an understanding of how as we increase awareness of our thoughts and experiences, we will be better able to intervene and make effective change.

CHAPTER SIX

Using Visualization to Achieve Greater Peace

"Yea, methought I saw, even as our father Lehi saw, God sitting upon his throne, surrounded with numberless concourses of angels, in the attitude of singing and praising their God; yea, and my soul did long to be there." (Alma 36:22)

Alma the Younger, the Book of Mormon prophet, had a rough start. He was the son of a prophet and his father's namesake. He was taught the truth from a young age, by example and precept. Yet Alma the Younger did not believe the things he had been taught. Instead, he chose a path of wickedness and rebellion. He was not content to revel in his own personal departure from the covenant path but felt compelled to get others to stray as well. As such, he and his band of rebels went about trying to convince church members to abandon the straight and narrow way and follow them in ways of wickedness. They were very successful in their endeavors. Their success caused great distress to their parents, who fasted and prayed for heavenly intervention to stop this pattern of destruction. Due to exceeding faith these prayers were answered in spectacular fashion. An angel of God, with a thunderous voice that shook the ground with each utterance, called Alma and his group to repentance. Alma was so overwhelmed that he was unconscious for three days. When he recovered, he repented and labored the rest of his days to repair the wrongs he had committed.

In later years, Alma described this experience to his son Helaman. He reviewed the three days he spent unconscious. Although his body was inert during that time, his mind was quite active, and it was something he never forgot. The initial part of his experience was genuine torment, as Alma described:

> Yea, I did remember all my sins and iniquities, for which I was tormented with the pains of hell; yea, I saw that I had rebelled against my God, and that I had not kept his holy commandments. Yea, and I had murdered many of his children, or rather led them away unto destruction; yea, and in fine so great had been my iniquities, that the very thought of coming into the presence of my God did rack my soul with inexpressible horror. Oh, thought I, that I could be banished and become extinct both soul and body, that I might not be brought to stand in the presence of my God, to be judged of my deeds. (Alma 36:13-15)

He was so distressed and frightened about his past sins that he wished for eternal extinction. He didn't just want to die; he wanted his body *and* soul to be eradicated, leaving no trace of existence. Of course, that was not possible. We are all responsible for our choices and will one day stand before God to account, whether we like it or not. In the midst of his suffering and terror, Alma remembered his father's teachings regarding the Savior and the promised redemption. He cried out in desperation, asking for forgiveness for his sins. When he did this, he received immediate relief from his pain. Ongoing repentance followed, but the liberation from his spiritual horror was instant. His mind was caught up in a heavenly scene showing the angelic abode of God. Alma remarks how he felt a strong desire to be there (see Alma 36:22). What a stark contrast from his previous emotion! Not long before this, Alma hoped he could become extinguished, so he wouldn't have to face God, yet in this moment he wanted nothing more than to be in His presence. The transformation was remarkable; such are the types of transformations made possible through the power of the Atonement of Jesus Christ.

Alma's mood varied dramatically depending upon the scene he envisioned. In the first instance, he saw himself facing an eventual appearance before God, guilty and convicted of horrible sins. The thought of having to be in such a setting caused incredible pain and agony. In the second instance, Alma saw himself standing before a loving and compassionate God. Alma pictured himself free from the burden of sin, having applied the mercies of the Savior extended to those who truly repent. The thought of being in such a setting caused great joy, to the point where he wanted to be there even then. That is a distinct difference: going from horror and avoidance to desire and longing. Curiously, the settings were both the same imagined place; they were both the presence of God. The difference was in how Alma viewed the potential experience. If God were a harsh judge and Alma was full of sin, the setting would have been frightening. If God were a merciful being and Alma was clean through the blood of Jesus, then the setting would have been welcoming. Alma's conception of the future changed his feelings in a marked fashion.

Anxiety responses tend to thrive on anticipated negative outcomes. It doesn't matter if the outcome has yet to occur; the associated emotion depends upon the person's view of the possible outcome. For example, say you are applying for a job. These situations bring most people a bit of anxiety, but the range of anxiety can vary greatly. You have an interview scheduled. Consider the two possible scenarios that follow, thinking about how your anticipation of events can affect the way you feel about them. Remember, these are not situations that have already happened, but just your perception of how you think the event might ultimately play out:

Scenario one: You feel very unsettled about the interview. You are not sure your qualifications will be sufficient for the job. You have heard that the person conducting the interviews is somewhat stern. As you think about possible outcomes, you see yourself having difficulty answering the interview questions. You envision the interviewer becoming frustrated with your performance, which increases your stress and worry. As your confidence decreases, you start to feel overwhelmed and on the verge of tears. The interview ends, you go out to your car, and the crying starts in earnest. For the next few days you are filled with fear and anxiety about your performance, beating yourself up for having performed so poorly. You eventually hear about the potential job offer: you didn't get it. Questions begin to flood your mind: *Why couldn't I even get through a single interview? What will I do now without a good job? How am I going to meet my financial responsibilities?* Anxiety grows as these questions linger in your mind with no resolution.

Scenario two: You feel confident about the interview. Although you are probably not the most qualified applicant, you are a quick learner and are motivated to do well. You have heard that the person conducting the interviews is somewhat stern. You think to yourself, "That's okay. I've dealt with stern people before. I may not like it that much, but I will do my best." You reflect on an answered prayer a few days earlier, where you felt confident the Lord would support you as you tried your best. As you think about possible outcomes, you see yourself answering the interview questions with poise. Although you are naturally somewhat nervous, you feel a calm assurance that things are going to work out. The interview ends, and you walk out with a feeling that you performed to the best of your ability. The next few days are filled with nervous anticipation, but also feelings of confidence. You eventually hear about the potential job offer: you didn't get it. Even though this is disappointing, you react with as much encouragement as you can. The following thoughts come to mind: *I did my best, and that's all I can do. I know the Lord will watch over me and bless me with what I need. I will continue to look for work, continue to develop my skills, and trust that things will work out.* A feeling of peace washes over you, along with a spiritual reassurance that your Heavenly Father loves you and is mindful of your situation.

Some readers may have expected a different outcome in scenario two. Perhaps you thought that situation would have resulted in you actually getting the job. After all, if we think positively, things will work out! Isn't that correct? Yes, I believe that is correct in almost all situations. What is incorrect is thinking that "things working out" means "I will not fail, I will not experience difficulty, I will not have heartache, etc." "Things working out" means things will happen according to the will of Father in Heaven, which often means a winding and occasionally frustrating path to eventual success.

Know that you can create feelings of fear *or* peace with the power of imagination. Remember, these scenarios were not things that had already happened. They were conceptions of the future that you created in your mind. Although the scenarios were fictitious, the feelings were real. The respective feelings of fear or peace were felt long before the job interview even happened, predicated upon your visualization of how the interview might work out. Visualization is a powerful tool to help manage our emotions but can be a two-edged sword when it comes to anxiety management. Visualization can serve to increase or decrease feelings of anxiety, depending upon how it is used. Here are two scriptural examples that illustrate this concept.

As Alma spoke to the church members in Zarahemla, he invited them to visualize their future meeting with God. He asked them to consider what that situation would be like, especially following a lifetime of good works. "Do you look forward with an eye of faith, and view this mortal body raised in immortality, and this corruption raised in incorruption, to stand before God to be judged according to the deeds which have been done in the mortal body? I say unto you, can you imagine to yourselves that ye hear the voice of the Lord, saying unto you, in that day: Come unto me ye blessed, for behold, your works have been the works of righteousness upon the face of the earth?" (Alma 5:15-16). What types of feelings would be caused by such an experience? I think whoever heard God speak the words "come unto me ye blessed" would be filled with joy, satisfaction, accomplishment, and eternal happiness. After all, we have come to this earth with the intention to return to our heavenly home, having completed the test of mortality. So many of us worry that we are not performing well, or we are somehow unacceptable to God. To have that final approval and come again into our Father's presence, never to depart, will be the most amazing experience. As Alma asked the people to visualize such a grand outcome, he was also inviting them to grow their feelings of faith, hope, and spiritual confidence.

Now consider another scriptural event, but with a different outcome. Moses had seen a dramatic vision, where he experienced the glory and power of God. He was told he was a son of God and that God had a specific plan for him. Moses was then shown all the inhabitants of the earth, which would have been incredible and even somewhat overwhelming to the physical senses. After the presence of God departed from Moses, he reflected on just how little and insignificant man was compared to the amazing splendor of the Almighty (see Moses 1:1-11). Immediately following this heavenly vision, Satan appeared to Moses. He challenged Moses' spiritual heritage, calling him a "son of man," and commanded Moses to worship him. Moses refused outright. He told Satan he could tell the difference between him and God, commented on the fact that Satan had no glory compared to Father in Heaven, and that he would have no more part of this preposterous conversation. This did not sit well with Satan, and he became angry. "And now, when Moses had said these words, Satan cried with a loud voice, and ranted upon the earth, and commanded, saying: I am the Only Begotten, worship me. And it came to pass that Moses began to fear exceedingly; and as he began to fear, he saw the bitterness of hell" (Moses 1:19-20). Seeing "the bitterness of hell" would certainly cause feelings of fear and dread. Satan's influence on Moses had the opposite effect of the Spirit. While the Spirit inspires feelings of peace, confidence and hope, the adversary promotes feelings of anxiety, mistrust and despair. Satan was trying to get Moses to envision a terrible outcome, even one where Satan ruled over him. That is the true bitterness of hell, where we have surrendered our agency to that being who seeks the misery of all mankind (see 2 Nephi 2:18).

In both of the preceding examples, the imagined event had not happened yet, but the feelings were real. Alma's followers were not yet in heaven, yet they were encouraged to envision this possibility and taste of the emotional experience that would accompany such an event. Moses was not in hell, but he was being tempted to visualize what that would be like and endure the associated feelings. *The way we think about the future can dramatically affect the way we feel about things in the present.* We have control over our thoughts, although it does take practice to learn how to manage them effectively.

I remember an experience many years ago that taught me the power of visualization and imagined outcomes. I have been self-employed as a psychologist for many years. While this has been a blessing in terms of work flexibility, it has also brought much anxiety at times. As those of you who are self-employed are aware, a steady paycheck is uncommon. Revenue varies from week to week. I often find myself worrying about how things are going to work out financially. I recall one occasion when I was driving home from work. At that time, the business was stable. I had sufficient referrals and things looked good into the distant future. Still, I found myself worried about what *might* happen. My thoughts included, "What if one of my contracts falls through? What if I get sick and cannot work? What if something happens to my psychology license and I cannot practice any longer?" None of those outcomes seemed even remotely likely at the time. The contracts appeared secure, my health was good and had been for some time, and I was consistent in doing those things that would preserve my license. Of course, accidents and other unanticipated events can happen, but I had no evidence to presume anything like that was on the horizon.

As I sat in the car and thought about these possible terrible outcomes, I was filled with anxiety. The future looked bleak. Yet in that moment I was blessed with some clarity. I remember thinking, "These feelings I'm having now; these are the feelings I *would naturally feel* if something really bad happened, like losing a contract or getting sick or losing my license. Yet in this moment, right now, I have stable contracts, good health, and a license in good standing. *Why am I spending this current moment full of anxiety and dread as if something bad had already happened?*" It was a stark revelation. Truly, at that time, things were good. If I chose, I could have sat back and enjoyed that experience for a moment, being thankful for what I had. Instead, I was all worked up about some unlikely future event. I was wasting the present moment, trading the peace I could rightly claim, for anxiety that was based on improbable outcomes. I looked at the clock; it was 5:44 p.m. As I attempted to calm my fears of the future and reduce the anxiety of the moment, I thought, "It's 5:44 p.m. Everything is good right now. Today, at 5:44 p.m., things are fine. Let's enjoy this moment. If everything goes horribly wrong at 5:45 p.m., then I will deal with that when it comes. But for now, 5:44 p.m. is going to be a good time."

Frank Waters, an American author, spoke of the concept of squandering the immediate moment in favor of past or future worries: "'I have no time!' This is the despairing cry of twentieth-century man, panicky with unrest, as he rushes ever faster from the past to the future over the knife-edge of the unlived present." [8] I have loved this quote for many years, although have had great difficulty employing the principle that it teaches. I often find myself spending too much of my present time either fretting over the past or worried about the future. In truth,

8 Frank Waters, *Frank Waters: A Respective Anthology*, ed. Charles Adams (Athens, Ohio: Swallow Press, 1985), 137.

there is nothing I can do about the past. Equally true, the future has not yet happened, and I cannot accurately predict what will occur. Why invest so much of my present energies into things I cannot change or control? When I think about it like this, it seems quite absurd. Yet it is challenging to manage in the moment. Just like that day in the car, things were good at 5:44 p.m. I needed to take the time to enjoy the peace of that moment. If you are curious about what happened at 5:45 p.m., I'll tell you. Nothing terrible happened. All was well. My life was the same as had been in the previous minute. In fact, if I recall correctly, things continued to go well for many months and years after that. There were challenges and setbacks, but nothing comparable to the desperate futures I was afraid of. Those dreaded futures, or visualized outcomes, caused anxiety in the moment. Yet they never happened like I feared they would. They still haven't happened.

People who experience anxiety tend to engage in this same practice quite often. Although things may be going well at any given time, they imagine unlikely future scenarios that fuel anxiety and destroy the chance for peace in the present. The following examples are fictional and perhaps overly dramatic, but they prove the point. See if you have ever found yourself having similar trains of thought:

Sure, my family is healthy now. But what if one of us gets some dread disease? What if it is a disease that has no cure? Or the cure is really expensive? What if it is so expensive that it exhausts all of our health insurance resources and we end up a million dollars in debt?

I know I have a good job now with a stable company. But what if the CEO is actually a scam artist and absconds with all of the company profits? What if all of us got laid off and there was no option for unemployment because of the CEO's fraud? We would blow through our meager savings and end up homeless, living on the streets.

Yes, I am aware that we currently have many resources at our disposal. But what if some crazy foreign nation starts a nuclear war and our country is wiped out? What if there are no more banks, stores, roads, or any sort of infrastructure? I mean, we have a little bit of food storage that is a couple decades old, but what about when we run out of that? We will all starve to death in a barren post-apocalyptic landscape.

I do not mean to make light of difficult situations. Bad things happen, and they are hard to deal with. Yet in my professional work, I encounter many people who get very creative in their dramatic and negative estimations of possible future events. If these are the types of thoughts that run through your head on a regular basis, you are going to have feelings of anxiety. I call this the "one-sided what-if" game. "What if" refers to the imagined scenarios: "*what if* such and such happens, etc." "One-sided" refers to the fact that the person does not give equal treatment to other possible, but equally unlikely scenarios. What if the person's future predictions were excessively positive instead of negative? Consider an alternate set of possibilities:

I understand I'm stuck in a dead-end job with limited prospects. But what if I discover a new cell phone technology that revolutionizes the world! I could license my ideas to all the major companies. Within a matter of weeks, I would become the world's first trillionaire and spend the rest of my days helping those who are less fortunate.

I am aware that my children have little motivation to do chores around the house. But what if I figure out a new, secret form of parenting that makes kids motivated all the time! My house would be clean every day, professors from universities around the world would come to seek my advice, and my schedule would be full of talk show appearances.

It's true that I often feel my friends don't listen to my opinion. But what if aliens came to visit and taught me intergalactic ways of being persuasive! I could wow my friends with compelling speeches. In addition, I'd show off the alien technology that I picked up in the teaching sessions aboard the mother ship. They don't listen to me much now, but they'd sure listen when I pull up next to their automobile in my teleporting spaceship!

These situations are ridiculous, right? Even a casual review would show the likelihood of these things happening is extremely remote, if not downright impossible. But say you had a friend who came to you with the first scenario, the one about cell phone technology. They told you their story and were giddy with anticipation. Then, they told you they had just applied for a 2.5 million dollar mortgage, bought five new cars, and leased a jet for all their upcoming meetings. They acknowledge they don't have any money right now, but the payments for these items wouldn't be due for another couple of months. By then they'll have their first few billion and things will be fine. As a good friend, you would probably do all you could to intervene and try to convince your friend to not make such extreme plans based on unlikely outcomes. After all, the things your friend hopes will come true have not happened, so it would be foolish to change current directions based on those expectations.

Can you see how this rationale applies to the other situations as well? If it is unreasonable for someone to buy cars and lease jets based on what *might happen* tomorrow, then isn't it just as unreasonable for someone to fear and panic based on what has not yet come to pass? When I deal with these issues in my psychology practice, I encourage the individual to take one of two approaches.

First approach: you need to be equal and fair in your unrealistic treatment of future events. If you insist on being anxious about some unlikely future catastrophe (horrible illness, financial devastation, nuclear annihilation), then you need to be just as hopeful about unlikely future successes (instant riches, miraculous cures, intergalactic influence). If you are going to play the "what if" game, you need to play it on both sides; make it a fair game. Let the fear of possible future loss be tempered by the joy of possible future gain. When someone asks how you are doing, you can genuinely say, "Well, tomorrow I may be in a supermax prison if everything goes horribly. Or, if everything goes amazingly I may be the leader of the free world. I guess you could say it's a mixed bag. It's hard to tell at this point."

Second approach: if you think it is ridiculous to walk around with a silly grin because tomorrow you might become the first interstellar trillionaire, then you should acknowledge it is equally unreasonable to walk around with a grimace because tomorrow you might be the most miserable person on the planet. Try to see the folly in both scenarios. Take a more measured approach to life, *accurately* weighing the good and the bad together. Don't exaggerate the negative and don't inflate the positive. Be an honest judge, looking objectively at all evidence, and then decide how to feel about the situation. If after a fair assessment, if the situation calls for anxiety, as some situations do, then go ahead and feel the anxiety. But if the situation does not call for anxiety, then try to resist the urge to feel that way.

How we visualize the future can have a significant impact in how we feel in the present. By doing your best to accurately and fairly visualize what might happen, you can mitigate feelings of anxiety. Also, you can build feelings of confidence by trying to visualize reasonable, positive outcomes. Because of the Atonement of Jesus Christ, hope can be the prevailing sentiment in our daily lives. There are always times when the future is going to look bleak, but we can change our perceptions and have greater trust in the Savior and His tremendous power to consecrate afflictions for our gain (see 2 Nephi 2:2).

Elder Jeffrey R. Holland told a story of embarking on a family move. He had a young family with two small children and had to travel almost three thousand miles across the country to begin graduate studies. His car broke down numerous times only after traveling a very short distance. After being helped by a friendly local, Elder Holland related the following: "'How far have you come?' [the local] said. 'Thirty-four miles,' I answered. 'How much farther do you have to go?' 'Twenty-six hundred miles,' I said. 'Well, *you* might make that trip, and *your wife* and those two little kiddies might make that trip, but *none of you* are going to make it in *that* car.' He proved to be prophetic on all counts." [9] Many years later, Elder Holland was traveling the same road. In his mind he imagined seeing his broken-down car and his young wife and children. He even imagined seeing himself walking towards town with much anxiety and distress. As if wanting to give advice to his younger self, Elder Holland continued, "In that imaginary instant, I couldn't help calling out to him: 'Don't give up, boy. Don't you quit. You keep walking. You keep trying. There is help and happiness ahead—a lot of it—30 years of it now, and still counting. You keep your chin up. It will be all right in the end. Trust God and believe in good things to come.'" [10]

Just like Elder Holland, there will be times in our lives when the future seems to hold nothing but trouble and fear. Yet the gospel of Jesus Christ is a gospel of hope; it is a gospel of happiness. "Men are that they might have joy" (2 Nephi 2:25). It is Satan who seeks our

9 Jeffrey R. Holland, "An High Priest of Good Things to Come," The Church of Jesus Christ of Latter-day Saints, November 1999, https://www.lds.org/ensign/1999/11/an-high-priest-of-good-things-to-come?lang=eng.

10 Ibid.

misery. We need to do all in our power to resist his temptations and fulfill the measure of our creation, which is to be like God and have the happiness that He possesses. That sort of happiness is not a distant dream but can be had *in this life* as we follow the Savior and faithfully strive to make and keep sacred covenants.

You can use visualization to see things in a more positive way and try to increase feelings of hope in your life. Here are some tips you can use to practice visualization. There are many ways to do this. No one way is "correct," but you should find what works for you. The outcome of successful visualization is greater peace and less anxiety. It will take practice and repeated attempts to achieve successful outcomes, so try to avoid frustration if you do not see immediate results. Be patient and consistent and the process will eventually bear fruit.

Prepare your setting. Similar to the instructions for meditation in the previous chapter, you need to do your best to find a setting that is free from distraction. Ideally you can find a place where you can lie down comfortably. Being physically comfortable is a key part of visualization, as physical discomfort can create distractions. Some may have circumstances where physical comfort is difficult to achieve, but all should try their best. The point is to try to find a setting that will maximize your comfort level, regardless of your situation.

Prepare your mind. During the visualization you will imagine a setting that is very peaceful. Prior to the experience, think about what your setting will be. Is it a setting in nature? Is it a favorite childhood location? Perhaps it is the celestial room of your favorite temple. The setting can be real or fictitious. However, you need to be able to provide a certain degree of detail in your mind when you visualize the setting. During the visualization you will also reflect on different statements that will provide peace. You should prepare these in advance. Some call these "affirmations." They can be statements like "I feel at peace" or "I am letting go of stress." I strongly suggest using scriptures as part of these affirmations. You can search the scriptures to find those that help you feel at peace and have greater faith. Some of my favorites are as follows:

"Be still, and know that I am God." (Psalm 46:10)

"Let not your heart be troubled, neither let it be afraid." (John

14:27)

"Walk in the meekness of my Spirit, and you shall have peace in me." (D&C 19:23)

Take some time to study the scriptures and find those verses which will give you peace. Make a note of them. If possible, commit them to memory. These scriptures and affirmations will play a large role in the visualization process.

Prepare your spirit. Before you begin your visualization, always start with prayer. Ask your Father in Heaven for what you need. Tell Him about your troubles and seek His guidance. Every psychological intervention and emotional cure will be enhanced as we seek the companionship of the Holy Ghost.

As you begin the actual visualization, do your best to follow these steps:

Find a comfortable position. If possible, find a place where you can lie down. Make sure you are wearing comfortable clothing. Try not to feel rushed or in a hurry to complete the task. Close your eyes and settle into the relaxation of peace and quiet.

Reduce physical tension. Starting with your head, focus on various body parts and see if they are tense. Go down your body in your mind, checking each major muscle group (neck, shoulders, chest, abdomen, etc.) and notice how you feel. If you feel tense in any area, try to relax those muscles.

Create a mental scene. Begin to imagine a place where you are at peace. This can be a place you have been before or perhaps a combination of favorite locations and images. As I've mentioned previously, I personally love the beach and have a favorite spot where I have sat in solitude and listened to the rhythm of the waves. Do your best to involve all of your senses as you think of this peaceful location. Imagine the sounds, smells, and sights. Is there a light breeze? Do the sun's rays feel warm on your face? What are the sounds? What are the sights? Is it a sunny day? Is it overcast? Is there a gentle rain? Remember, this is *your* special place; it can be anything you want. Create that place in your mind using your imagination. Add as many pleasant and peaceful elements as you'd like and eliminate all distractions. Once you have fully imagined your calm setting, lie there and enjoy the peace and serenity.

Use positive affirmations. As we discussed before, this is the time where you can repeat short, positive statements that will help you achieve greater peace. I highly recommend using scriptures as part of this process. If you can commit the scripture to memory, either verbatim or a close version, that will help. Go over those verses in your mind. Review any other affirmations as well. Try to resist thoughts that might counter your calming statements. Let those negative thoughts pass by while you refocus your mind on the positive and peaceful assertions you have previously studied and prepared.

Conclude slowly and intentionally. Similar to the meditation practice, most won't have unlimited time and resources to visualize for extended periods of time. I think of the busy mother who may have to move heaven and earth just to find five undisturbed minutes. If you are able, then visualize for as long as it feels good and brings peace. If you do not have that type of time or flexibility in your schedule, then visualize for as much time as you can. As you approach the end of your visualization, take time to slowly bring yourself back to reality. Even though this may be an unpleasant thought for some, be grateful for the time you were able to spend in peace and solitude while in your place of serenity.

End with prayer. After you are done with your visualization, thank Heavenly Father for the chance to do this. Express gratitude for the peace you felt. Ask for the companionship of the Holy Ghost, the true Comforter, to be with you always. Seek your Father in Heaven's guidance for what you can do in order to have greater peace and harmony in your life.

Just as with meditation, learning to effectively practice visualization will take time and effort. Try not to be frustrated if your initial attempts are unsuccessful. Visualization is a skill, and just like any skill, you'll become better at it as you practice it over and over. Don't forget to ask for heavenly assistance to build your abilities in this area. God loves you and will bless you with the righteous desires of your heart.

Practical suggestions for change:

Begin a practice of regular visualization following the outlined principles.

Develop an understanding of how the way we foresee future events, either positively or negatively, can have an effect on the emotions we feel in the present.

CHAPTER SEVEN

Changing Thought Patterns Changes Emotional Reactions

"For as he thinketh in his heart, so is he." (Proverbs 23:7)

The "war chapters" in the Book of Mormon have always been interesting to me. When I was younger I thought perhaps Mormon included them because of his personal military connections. As I have become older, I have found so many life lessons and gospel truths in these chapters that I am convinced the primary reason for their inclusion was to teach eternal principles. Captain Moroni was the head captain of the Nephite armies at this time. His armies were vastly outnumbered by their Lamanite enemies. Yet through strategy and reliance on the Lord, the Nephites won most battles and kept possession of critical cities and strongholds. At one point in their history, Moroni felt pleased with the progress of his armies. Still, he worried there weren't enough of them to effectively maintain the ground they had taken. He sent word to the Nephite government to provide additional troops to strengthen the his armies and enable them to remain victorious.

However, when the reinforcements arrived, they were few in number and a very small percentage of the overall available military force. Moroni and his chief captains started to wonder why so few troops had been sent by the government. In the meantime, the Lamanites attacked and took possession of several key strongholds, which frustrated Moroni. So much of the work his armies had recently accomplished was eroding because of the lack of government support. Moroni made another desperate plea to the government to send more troops. This time, his request apparently fell on deaf ears. No additional troops were sent, and the Nephites sustained more losses. Moroni became frustrated to the point of anger. "And it came to pass that Moroni was angry with the government, because of their indifference concerning the freedom of their country" (Alma 59:13). He wrote a scathing letter of rebuke to the Nephite chief executive, Pahoran, basically calling him a traitor. Moroni essentially threatened Pahoran's life and told him that if he did not repent of his slothful and evil ways, he would bring his armies to the Nephite capital and fight Pahoran and his followers to the point of extinction.

You can see the connection between Moroni's thought patterns and his emotions in the verse just mentioned. To paraphrase, Moroni's thoughts were: *The government doesn't care about freedom. They don't care about us. They are willing to let us die while we fight for their safety.* These thoughts led to the resulting emotion: "Moroni was angry with the government." This makes sense; Moroni's anger seems like a very natural reaction to the situation as he perceived it.

Moroni eventually received a return correspondence from Pahoran, in response to his heavy-handed threat. Pahoran explained his grief for Moroni's situation. He stated that an opposing faction had arisen in the Nephite capital, who had sympathized with the enemy and were trying to unite with them. This faction had also intimidated those who would otherwise go and fight with the Nephite armies, resulting in no troops being sent to Moroni's aid. Pahoran stated he was in exile, uncertain of what to do. However, after reading Moroni's letter he became convinced that military action was needed against the growing group of traitors. Moroni quickly responded to Pahoran's request. He marched on the Nephite capital, gaining support as he went. Once he arrived, his armies quickly dispensed with the defectors. He recruited many thousands of soldiers to return to the battlefield. They were ultimately victorious, not only against the factions at home, but also against their enemies in surrounding lands. The Nephites won the war, and Moroni retired in peace.

After Moroni received Pahoran's letter, the scriptures record his reaction as follows: "And now it came to pass that when Moroni had received this epistle his heart did take courage, and was filled with exceedingly great joy because of the faithfulness of Pahoran, that he was not also a traitor to the freedom and cause of his country" (Alma 62:1). Notice the considerable difference in Moroni's reaction! Just some time earlier he was very angry, believed Pahoran was a traitor, and was ready to wipe him out. Yet after receiving the letter, Moroni had "exceedingly great joy" because of Pahoran. What changed? Moroni's perception of the situation changed, which subsequently changed his emotions and attitude. Again, see the connection between Moroni's thoughts and his emotions. To paraphrase his revised thoughts: *The government does support us; they are simply under attack themselves. They have supported us all along. They are not traitors and need our help.* These thoughts led to Moroni's feelings of exceeding joy; essentially the opposite of his previous feelings of anger.

These types of situations happen every day of our lives. We experience something, form an opinion about it, and have an emotional reaction. As we have discussed before, we can't always control our experiences. Moroni had no control over whether a rebellion would arise; it simply happened, and he was left to deal with the aftermath. Moroni *did* have control over how he perceived and thought about this situation. When he believed the government was complicit in the process, he was angry and threatening. When he believed the government was a victim of the process, he was hopeful and motivated. He could not change the circumstances, but he could change the way he thought about the circumstances.

This type of intervention is key in managing anxiety. We cannot typically change the events that happen in our lives. Random things occur; many situations are far outside of our control. We live in a world where we are affected by the choices of billions of others. With anxiety management, we essentially have two places we can intervene. We can either try to change the events that happen in life, or we can change the way we think about these events. I have known many people who regularly choose the first option; they try to manage their life events so that nothing anxiety-provoking will happen. These are some of the most frustrated and exhausted people I know. In Chapter One we reviewed the story of the Savior on the Sea of Galilee as He calmed the tempest. We talked about how ineffective it is for us to try to calm the waves or stop the wind from blowing. The more effective approach involves thinking differently about the storm, which involves having faith that storms eventually blow over, doing your part to navigate to the best of your ability, and believing that when you are sailing with the Lord of heaven and Earth you are not going to perish.

Effective anxiety management involves changing the way we think about events. I have had many personal and professional experiences with this process. As an example, I remember working with a person many years ago. When he was younger, he had been the victim of significant abuse at the hand of his father. The person was much older now. His dad was in prison, yet my friend continued to experience much emotional pain and grief because of the abuse. One day he asked me, "How can I stop feeling this pain?" I told him, in my estimation, the best way for him to stop feeling the pain was to forgive his father. He responded, "I will *never* forgive him for what he did to me." I replied that I completely understood. It was his right to withhold forgiveness. What had been done to him was unconscionable. Yet I restated my position. Regardless of whether his father deserved forgiveness or whether my friend was in the right to withhold forgiveness, the path to greater happiness was clear: he needed to forgive his father. As far as I know, he never did. We parted ways and I have not heard from him. I truly hope he has done what is needful to be at peace.

This is another situation that highlights the relationship between events and emotions, along with the power of how such events are perceived. The event was the abuse; the emotion was pain and grief. For those who have been in similar situations, they know that there is power, healing, and hope that comes from learning to forgive and move on. Forgiveness does not change the past; it merely changes one's perception, which then results in a new emotional experience. If my friend had changed the way he thought about his abusive past, he could have had a different emotional outcome. So many people feel they are victims to their emotions, having no control over them. This is simply untrue. The way we feel about things will absolutely change as we modify the way we think about things.

Anxiety often thrives on what are called "cognitive distortions." Cognitive distortions are patterns of thought that have been developed over time but that are untrue. They exert influence in the second link in the chain of event, belief, and emotion. The reason they are problematic is because they are untrue. They cause emotional reactions that are not necessarily indicated for the situation. They are common and happen to everyone. In the example of Captain Moroni, the cognitive distortion was his belief that the government was unsupportive and traitorous. To better understand this concept, let's consider another scriptural example, this one from the life of Enoch the prophet. Before he was called as a prophet, the scriptures record he journeyed in the land. One day, the Spirit came to him and informed him he would become a prophet of God. I imagine Enoch's reaction was similar to all prophets upon receiving their call. He was likely overwhelmed, humbled, and worried. He replied to the Lord, "Why is it that I have found favor in thy sight, and am but a lad, and all the people hate me; for I am slow of speech; wherefore am I thy servant?" (Moses 6:31).

As we apply the cognitive distortion model to this situation, the "event" was the calling to be a prophet. The "emotion" was feeling overwhelmed. Now let's analyze the "belief" that followed the event and contributed to the emotion. Please permit me a little bit of psychologist license to estimate why Enoch may have felt the way he did. In the aforementioned scripture, Enoch mentioned three things as part of his belief:

"I am but a lad": Scholars believe Enoch may have been as old as 65 at the time he received his call. I recognize people lived much longer back then, but calling yourself a "lad" at 65 years of age seems odd by today's standards. Perhaps he was referring more to his perceived inexperience. We truly don't know, but what we do know is he thought himself unqualified.

"I am slow of speech": I suppose we don't know much about this. Maybe he was a poor public speaker and worried about how he would communicate the word of God to the people.

"All the people hate me": this one is my favorite, only because it shows just how human we can all be at times. I'm certain Enoch felt particularly overwhelmed in this moment and was focused on his faults and weaknesses to the exclusion of his good traits. Surely there were one or two people on the face of the earth that were friends with Enoch. In fact, he probably had many friends and associates. This humble servant of God was likely so stunned that his innate reaction was to possibly exaggerate the true nature of any social liabilities.

God's response is remarkable and comforting: "Go forth and do as I have commanded thee, and no man shall pierce thee. Open thy mouth, and it shall be filled, and I will give thee utterance, for all flesh is in my hands, and I will do as seemeth me good.... Behold my Spirit is upon you, wherefore all thy words will I justify; and the mountains shall flee before you, and the rivers shall turn from their course; and thou shalt abide in me, and I in you; therefore walk with me" (Moses 6:32, 34). Can you see the Lord's responses to Enoch's concerns? "I am but a lad" is met with, "No man shall pierce thee." In other words: *I'll take care of you. I will compensate for your perceived inexperience and shortcomings.* "I am slow of speech" is countered with, "Open thy mouth, and it shall be filled, and I will give thee utterance." In other words: *Don't worry about your speaking ability. You are my servant and I will put words in your mouth.* "All the people hate me" is reassured through, "Thou shalt abide in me, and I in you; therefore walk with me." In other words: *Even if everyone does hate you, I don't. You've got at least one friend out there, and that's me.* Enoch went on to become a powerful prophet who literally led his people to heaven (see Moses 7:69).

Let's look at other examples of cognitive distortions that are likely more common to our experience. Say you are required to complete some task. It could be anything: raising children, doing a church calling, enduring a trial, taking a final exam, teaching a lesson, etc. Here are some common beliefs that often surface when we have a task to perform:

1. I'm not good at anything.
2. I fail whenever I try to do something.
3. Everyone will make fun of my performance.
4. I'm not strong enough to do it.

Each of these beliefs will lead to feelings of worry, inadequacy, failure and anxiety. Now, consider some modifications to these beliefs that will result in changes to the accompanying emotions:

1. There are some things I'm not good at, but others I am. I can work to increase my skills in areas where I'm weak.
2. I have failed in the past at some things, but I have succeeded at others.
3. Some people will probably not like what I do, but there are

others who will support me and help me along.

4. I may not be strong enough to do this, but I can request help from friends, family and the Lord to get the strength to finish the task.

Each of these beliefs will lead to feelings of encouragement, hope, and increased resolve. In addition, the second set of beliefs is more accurate than the first set of beliefs. Most of the time, cognitive distortions are inaccurate because they are global and negative. They tend to use words like always, never, everyone, or no one. We need to learn to identify and correct cognitive distortions in order to develop better anxiety management strategies.

One of the key strategies in changing longstanding thinking patterns is to seek the guidance of the Holy Ghost. Secular psychology strategies can be effective, but they are always enhanced when we use the Spirit as our teacher. Consider these teachings from the prophet Jacob. We have already reviewed how he used spiritual means to help manage anxiety issues. "Behold, my brethren, he that prophesieth, let him prophesy to the understanding of men; for the Spirit speaketh the truth and lieth not. Wherefore, *it speaketh of things as they really are, and of things as they really will be*; wherefore, these things are manifested unto us plainly, for the salvation of our souls" (Jacob 4:13, emphasis added).

"Things as they really are" and "things as they really will be" suggests an accurate analysis of what is truly happening in our lives. The Spirit is able to cut through the falsehoods, deceptions, and incorrect thinking that often contribute to excessive anxiety. As you work on changing your thought processes, remember to ask for help from your Father in Heaven. He will send the companionship of the Holy Ghost which will enhance your abilities to identify and cling to truth, while shedding false notions.

Notwithstanding the help of the Spirit, identifying cognitive distortions takes practice. It will take time and effort to learn to do this effectively. Usually we don't recognize our thoughts unless we have developed a habit of this. In most situations, we recognize our emotions first because they tend to be powerful and unmistakable. In the case of anxiety, the feeling of fear or apprehension is probably the first clue that we have recently had a thought or belief that caused the anxiety reaction. Here is a process you can follow to help understand and correct cognitive distortions. It is often helpful to write down your experiences and thoughts. Let's discuss the process and then go through it with an actual experience from my life.

Describe the situation. After a particularly anxiety-provoking experience, take a step back and describe what happened. What was the day like? Did anything out of the ordinary occur? Approximately when did the anxiety begin? What was happening at the time? Try to remember as much detail as you can. As you do this over and over with similar experiences, you may start to notice patterns.

Describe your thoughts. Analyze your thinking about the situation. What judgments did you make? What conclusions did you reach? What are your beliefs about what happened? This may be somewhat difficult to do at first as it requires the ability to think about your thinking. Don't worry; practice and experience will make the process easier over time.

Describe your feelings. This step is probably the easiest of them all. What did you feel? How long did the feelings last? Try to be as detailed as possible in this step. Don't just say "I felt anxiety." Take a close look at your feelings and include all derivatives of the anxious response, including others that may have not been anxiety related (such as anger, depression, etc.).

Scrutinize your thinking. This is where the work of change begins. Up until this point you have only been describing your experience. Now you have the chance to challenge your thinking. Consider the thoughts you described in the second step. What inaccuracies can you find? In what ways are they extreme or untrue? You could make a list of "accurate elements" and "inaccurate elements" that relate to the thoughts. Most beliefs are not completely true or completely false; there are elements of each in both.

Search for doctrine. Once you have identified the belief(s) associated with your anxiety response, search the scriptures and words of living prophets for truths that have been taught on the subject. This may take some time. If you have gone through this process before, you may already have a number of gospel truths identified on a certain topic. Write down quotes from scripture, general conference and other trustworthy sources that are based in truth. See if you can explain the truth in your own words as well.

Identify accurate beliefs. For the final step, review the thoughts you came up with in step two. Most of the time, these thoughts will have some level of inaccuracy. Rewrite these thoughts so they are more accurate. Use these newly considered thoughts as a blueprint for future anxiety experiences. Try to replace your old, inaccurate thoughts with these new beliefs. *This will take time.* Although our brains are very willing to change and accept new information, they also need much repetition and consistency to adapt.

Let's look at a recent example from my own life and apply this process.

As previously mentioned, I have been self-employed for almost my entire career. As such, I am responsible for arranging my own retirement. While I truly hope Social Security will still be around after I retire, I have tried to plan so that we will have sufficient reserves just in case. One day I received a letter from my financial planner. It had details regarding our retirement fund. I looked at the total amount invested. Then I foolishly typed "how much do I need to retire" in a Google search. I did some quick mental calculations, estimated future income, and then started to feel a dramatic increase in anxiety. For the rest of the day I was anxious, worried about how long I'd have to work, whether we'd be able to retire early enough to serve missions, and similar concerns. I talked about it with my wife, who has always had more faith than I have had. She told me she was not concerned in the least, as the Lord has always provided for us. I tried to adopt her belief but was not successful; my stress and anxiety continued. I went to bed anxious and concerned.

The next morning, I felt a little better, but still had lingering concerns. As I left for work with a heavy heart, my wife said, "I prayed for you that you'd feel less stressed." I arrived at work and began the day as usual. At that point in my career, a good portion of my practice involved business with the local welfare department. They would send many clients every week for a brief psychological evaluation. These were individuals who had applied for government assistance, claiming they were unable to work due to psychological difficulties. My job was to evaluate their psychological functioning and determine whether it impacted their work abilities or not. I did many such evaluations each week. That particular day, I had a full schedule of these evaluations.

My first client of the day arrived. He had a large backpack with a sleeping bag attached. He had a few other bags, fully stuffed, that he carried with him. He was dirty and disheveled. It had been somewhat rainy in the area of late, and he smelled like old, wet clothing. It was clear that not only had he been living on the streets for quite some time, but that he had every earthly possession he owned with him in my office. We sat down and started talking about his history. I asked him what mental health issues he had that might prevent him from being able to work. He stated he had a history of anxiety and depression. While the anxiety was still fairly high, the depression had alleviated a bit over time. He then went on to explain that each day, he tried to think of the good things happening in his life. As he did this with consistency, in time he found the depression symptoms were less and less. We continued to explore anxiety symptoms, but part of my mind was very much caught up in his previous disclosures. Eventually we ended the interview and parted ways.

I was thunderstruck with feelings of guilt, remorse, and shame. For the past 24 hours I had been worried about our financial situation. I was worried about being able to retire in a timely fashion. I felt as if I wasn't being given a fair shake, looking at others around me and believing somehow their situation was more favorable. Then I was absolutely schooled by a homeless, destitute man who had been truly managing feelings of depression by thinking about "all the good things" in his life. I immediately dropped to my knees and apologized to my Father in Heaven for being so selfish and myopic. I expressed gratitude for the multitude of blessings I had. I texted my wife and told her, "Your prayer worked." The Lord knows how to teach me in ways I am likely to learn. Better than having me remember a favorite scripture or conference talk, he brought someone to my office to help me see things more clearly. It was an experience I will never forget.

Now let's apply the six-step process to this situation. How did I go from anxiety to peace? How can I avoid similar situations in the future?

Step one: describe the situation. Here is what happened: I had received a retirement financial summary. I looked up how much I should have to retire. I compared the two numbers and started to think about potential shortfalls.

Step two: describe your thoughts. Here are the thoughts I had: "It doesn't appear I'm saving enough money, yet I don't have any more to save. I'm going to have to work much longer than I thought. This is going to impact our ability to serve missions. We may not be able to travel as much and visit children and grandchildren. Other people seem to be making less but saving more. I never should have chosen self-employment as an option. Perhaps if I had gone into a different profession, I'd have a more secure retirement. Social Security is likely to go bankrupt and that is going to seriously affect our ability to make ends meet after retirement. I may have to continue working for the rest of my life."

Step three: describe your feelings. Here are the feelings I had: "I feel anxious. I feel worried. I feel upset. I feel regret."

Step four: scrutinize your thinking. Here is a critical analysis of my thoughts: "I just met a man who has almost nothing, yet he has more peace and hope than I do in the moment. He was grateful for the things he has. I am focusing on the things I don't have to the exclusion of the abundance I've been given by the Lord. Self-employment has been a great blessing. The Lord has always provided for our needs and for many of our wants as well. I am healthy and able to work. I have no idea if things would have been better in traditional employment, if Social Security will go bankrupt, or if others are able to save more than I can. I have the power to keep my covenants and exercise obedience to the commandments. I need to show greater appreciation for the things I do have and continue to trust in my loving and compassionate Father in Heaven."

Step five: search for doctrine. The following scriptures came to mind:

"For thus saith the Lord—I, the Lord, am merciful and gracious unto those who fear me, and delight to honor those who serve me in righteousness and in truth unto the end. Great shall be their reward and eternal shall be their glory." (D&C 76:5-6)

"And I, Enos, knew it would be according to the covenant which he had made; wherefore my soul did rest." (Enos 1:17)

"But Alma went forth and stood among them, and exhorted them that they should not be frightened, but that they should remember the Lord their God and he would deliver them. Therefore they hushed their fears..." (Mosiah 23:27-28)

"Therefore, fear not, little flock; do good; let earth and hell combine against you, for if ye are built upon my rock, they cannot prevail." (D&C 6:34)

What does this doctrine teach me? It teaches that the Lord fulfills His promises. It teaches that He loves me. It teaches that He will fight my battles if I will be faithful to my covenants. It teaches that I have the power to calm my anxieties. It teaches that there is nothing so daunting or difficult that I cannot beat it if I partner with the Savior.

Step six: Identify accurate beliefs. Now that I have been able to identify the thoughts that led to anxiety, identify some of the flaws in that thinking, and find doctrine that supports a clearer view of the situation, I'm ready to modify my beliefs so that they are more accurate. Here are some examples of beliefs that address the situation but are not as inaccurate as the ones previously expressed:

"The Lord wants me and my wife to serve missions; if I work to the best of my ability and keep His commandments, He will provide a way."

"My profession has allowed me to help many people and feel the Spirit as I do this. The Lord knows how long I will work and serve others; He will ensure I have the capacities to do it."

"I truly don't know the financial situations of other people. It is unreasonable to compare a true knowledge of my own situation to a guess about the situations of others."

"Making wild estimations about the future, such as the potential state of the Social Security system, will just lead me into faithless worry. The Lord has all power. He loves me. He blesses those who keep their covenants with those things they need. I just have to do my best and keep my covenants; the Lord will clear the way for the rest."

Some may say, *Well, that's easy for you to say, but it's much harder to put those beliefs into practice if you've held opposing beliefs for so many years.* First, let me assure you, these things are *not* easy for me to say.

They run contrary to many of my natural, faithless instincts. Yet I have learned to try to identify truth and incorporate it into my life. It has taken years and years of practice. Quite frankly, it has only been recently that I've started to see some significant results. I'm not suggesting this process will be easy. On the contrary, I know it will be very difficult. In fact, I hope it will be very difficult for all who attempt it. Easily accomplished tasks do not typically yield enduring benefits. The long-lasting and character-building experiences of life come from hard-fought, difficult processes that often go on for years. As you are able to change your thinking and develop greater control over anxiety, I want you to look back on your experiences. I want you to see just how much you fought and how hard you worked. Surveying the valley floor from the mountaintop is all the sweeter when you remember each painful step, each drop of sweat, and each effort-filled moment that was part of your ascent.

Elder David A. Bednar provided the following counsel: "Trust and confidence in Christ and a ready reliance on His merits, mercy, and grace lead to hope, through His Atonement, in the Resurrection and eternal life (see Moroni 7:41). Such faith and hope invite into our lives the sweet peace of conscience for which we all yearn. The power of the Atonement makes repentance possible and quells the despair caused by sin; it also strengthens us to see, do, and become good in ways that we could never recognize or accomplish with our limited mortal capacity." [11]

With consistent practice, over time you will become better at recognizing your thoughts, identifying those aspects that are inaccurate, and adopting modified thoughts that are truer and rooted in gospel doctrine. As you are able to do this, you will achieve a greater measure of the "sweet peace of conscience" referred to by Elder Bednar.

Practical suggestions for change:

Start becoming more aware of your experiences, thoughts, and feelings using the outlined principles.

Accept the fact that you can change your thought patterns through consistent, dutiful effort.

---

11 David A. Bednar, "Therefore They Hushed Their Fears," *Ensign,* May 2015, 47.

CHAPTER EIGHT

Greater Coping Strategies Increase Anxiety Tolerance

"But he that shall endure unto the end, the same shall be saved." (Matthew 24:13)

Some of you are familiar with the concept of a Latter-day Saint "trek" activity. In the mid-1800s, members of The Church of Jesus Christ of Latter-day Saints fled persecution in Illinois. They assembled in companies and traveled over 1200 miles, mostly by foot, to what would become Salt Lake City and the state of Utah. It was an arduous experience fraught with suffering and death. Modern members of the Church believe it is important to understand, even to a small degree, what these individuals went through. To this end, small "treks" are often held during the summer. Youth ranging from ages 12-18 will pack a limited amount of camping gear, don pioneer clothing, and travel to a remote location where they will push and pull wooden handcarts for several days across difficult terrain. For some of these youth, it becomes the most difficult physical experience they have ever had. Leaders plan these events to help the youth have an authentic experience, complete with hardship and personal trials.

My wife and I had the opportunity to be adult leaders on a trek some years ago. We were assigned a small group of youth, called our "family," and we were respectively "Ma" and "Pa." We loaded all our gear into a handcart and pushed and pulled it over hills, flats, water crossings, and other terrain. Our job was to help the youth remain motivated. This was pretty easy the first day, as we were all fresh, excited and full of energy. Our job grew more difficult as the days went on. I remember one youth in particular. He was a good young man, with emphasis on "young." He was only twelve years of age, was small in stature, and was clearly not accustomed to hard physical labor. He endured well the first couple of days, but by the third and final day, he was clearly exhausted. The shoes he brought were insufficient for the task and he had multiple blisters on his feet. We did our best to provide first aid, but each step for him was clearly painful. We had two water crossings that day, which meant his poor shoes and socks were soaked, increasing his discomfort. After the second water crossing, he walked to a small tree and sat on the ground.

I felt so sorry for this poor youth. I was sore and tired as well and could only imagine the grief he was going through. In addition to his physical pain, he was homesick and had truly had enough of this trek. I went over to talk with him. I told him we were on the last day and probably only had a couple more hours of walking until we were finished. Good food, family and friends awaited us. He looked at me and said, "I'm done." I knew he was serious. I looked around at where we were. We were in the middle of nowhere. It was flat, barren, and hot. There were a few handcarts passing by, pulled by youth who were similarly exhausted. They mustered smiles as they saw the two of us, but they were at their emotional ends as well. To be honest, I was a little bit "done" myself. The prior two days had been very difficult. I was ready for a good meal, hot shower, and comfortable bed. There was only one problem; none of those things were available in our current location. In order to get to those things, we had to keep walking.

I told this youth, "I know how you feel. I'm tired too. But at this point, we don't have many options. There is only one way out of here, and that's to keep walking to the end. We will make it! It will be difficult, but we will make it." With some emotional encouragement and me literally pulling him up off the ground, we resumed our march. As we both hoped and expected, in a few hours we arrived at the end. As promised, there were friends, family, and delicious food. He fell into the arms of his waiting mother, sobbing. I shed a tear or two myself realizing what he had done. I hoped it would be something he would always remember.

While our three-day trek was a small taste of what the pioneers experienced in their months-long expedition, so their westward migration was a small taste of what we all experience in our journey through life.

We left our home in heaven and came to a place we had never been before. We hope to get back to where we started. In the meantime, there are trials, difficulties, stressors, pitfalls, and everything else we can imagine complicating our way. There have been many times when I have figuratively sat on the ground in the middle of life's road, saying "I'm done. I can't go any farther. My feet hurt, I'm tired, and I don't have energy for another step." Maybe you've been there as well. I can say that every time I've done that, the eventual outcome has been the same. Ultimately, I get back up and keep walking. I imagine you've had similar experiences.

Why do we keep going in such circumstances? Probably for the same reasons that my young friend and I got up, dusted ourselves off, and kept walking after that final water crossing. First, there weren't a lot of options at that point. I suppose we could have tried to make a life for ourselves in that forsaken part of central Washington, but he had the rest of summer break to look forward to and I had to get back to work on Monday. Moving forward was our best bet, even though it was difficult. Also, I think we both realized that continuing the journey was the right thing to do. I don't think we ever *seriously* considered stopping for good, as we knew there was greater happiness ahead if we just kept going. That perspective helped us both to dig deep, find additional motivation, and move forward despite our pain.

Life's difficulties often catch us by surprise. I was pretty excited to go on the trek. Perhaps my young friend was also. In fact, I remember seeing a lot of smiles that first day as we traveled to the starting point and saw the handcarts. I remember seeing fewer and fewer smiles as the days went on. Thankfully, the smiles returned upon finishing the journey. I wonder if our mortal experience is similar. We know we shouted for joy upon hearing the details of the plan of salvation (see Job 38:7). I'll bet we waited with significant anticipation for our chance to come to Earth, gain physical bodies, and experience the trials that would help us become more like God. Then we finally arrived. The first few years were blissful, with people carrying us places, feeding us and paying our rent. We thought the teenage years were rough, but that's because we hadn't experienced adult trials yet. Then we finally hit adulthood, with some going on to marriage and parenting. We all collectively thought, "Are you serious? *This* is what I waited for?" All of the sudden, life became very difficult! With each hill to climb and each new blister, we wanted to just sit down and stop.

I have noticed an increasing tendency in society, where "sitting down and stopping" has become more and more acceptable. If something becomes too difficult, just don't do it any longer! The idea of perseverance in the face of challenges is declining, and more people are simply giving up in such situations. I encountered this issue with a former client. He was a youth that was almost eighteen years of age. He had impulse control problems and some mild learning disabilities. He did not enjoy school and was not looking forward to a career. I knew he had abilities and would certainly be able to do *something* productive to support himself. However, he and his family were convinced otherwise. We worked together for a few months and progress was limited. Eventually he moved to another state. A few months later I received a letter from that state's welfare agency. They wanted me to detail this young man's liabilities, so they could certify him as disabled and he could start receiving government payments. I wrote a return letter stating this young man did have certain liabilities, but he was absolutely capable of working. I never heard back from the agency or the young man. I wasn't about to be complicit in creating a scenario that could limit his personal growth and eventual happiness. I knew it would be a challenge for him, but that didn't concern me in the least. The challenge is what creates a growth opportunity.

I'm not suggesting everyone out there is capable of everything they set their mind to. We all have different abilities and sometimes they limit our overall capacities. To this point, I have worked with the developmentally delayed for most of my career. Some of them have significant disabilities that make even simple tasks very difficult for them to perform. Even with this understanding, I have always insisted they try to do as much as they are capable of. Developing an accurate estimation of our abilities and then working as diligently as possible to maximize our efforts is key in being able to cope with the anxiety that comes from life's challenges.

Coping strategies are exercises or methods we use in order to deal with stressful events. They can be negative or positive. For example, let's say you just found out you are going to lose your job. A positive coping strategy might be to talk with friends to process your emotions. A negative coping strategy might be to avoid any conversation about it and pretend it is not going to happen. Positive coping strategies come in many different forms, take practice, and can be easily adapted to individual needs. Frankly, anything that helps you solve a problem, process emotions, or move forward without causing damage to yourself or others could be considered a positive coping strategy. The following are two different coping strategies one can use to help manage anxiety and stress.

Gain greater perspective regarding stressful events

One coping strategy professionals recommend for anxiety management is to have individuals create a list of stressful events, beginning with mild stress and ending with extreme stress. For example, if someone had social anxiety, their list might begin with something like "being in a group of two to three people" and ending with "having to give an extemporaneous speech in front of one thousand people," with various other scenarios in between. As the person and the professional discuss these issues, they come to conclusions regarding how the person could actually cope with the various situations. They explore the feelings and thoughts related to the stressful experiences. They consider behaviors and principles that could help in such settings. This process tends to provide insight which hopefully reduces overall anxiety about the various events on the list.

Would you believe the Lord did something similar with Joseph Smith, during a time in the Prophet's life when his stress was fairly high? Joseph was unjustly incarcerated in the Liberty Jail in Missouri from December 1838 to April 1839. Conditions in the jail were deplorable and the prisoners truly suffered. During this time the Saints were stripped of the company and leadership of their prophet, which caused emotional and spiritual suffering among them as well. At one point during his incarceration, Joseph cried out, "O God, where art thou? And where is the pavilion that covereth thy hiding place? How long shall thy hand be stayed, and thine eye, yea thy pure eye, behold from the eternal heavens the wrongs of thy people and of thy servants, and thine ear be penetrated with their cries?" (D&C 121:1-2) Truly this was a stressful time for the Prophet. In response to his pleas for help and divine assistance, the Lord provided comfort. However, it was not in the manner we all might desire if in a similar situation. Joseph may have wanted a heavenly rescue or assurances that the Saints had been delivered. Instead, the Lord provided a list of things that could *further* go wrong in the Prophet's life, things that would only serve to increase anxiety and stress. Let's review Doctrine and Covenants section 122, verses five through nine:

"If thou art called to pass through tribulation; if thou art in perils among false brethren; if thou art in perils among robbers; if thou art in perils by land or by sea;" (D&C 122:5)

With this, the Lord begins a recitation of things that could go wrong in Joseph's life. Notice the content of the very first sentence, "If thou art called to pass through tribulation." It doesn't say "if trouble happens to find you" or "if through the random course of life, you happen to get into some deep water." It suggests the Lord is holding the reins and that sometimes, He calls us to pass through trials and tribulations. This verse goes on to refer to people conspiring against Joseph, false brethren and robbers trying to destroy his peace. Then the Lord continues:

"If thou art accused with all manner of false accusations; if thine enemies fall upon thee; if they tear thee from the society of thy father and mother and brethren and sisters; and if with a drawn sword thine enemies tear thee from the bosom of thy wife, and of thine offspring, and thine elder son, although but six years of age, shall cling to thy garments, and shall say, My father, my father, why can't you stay with us? O, my father, what are the men going to do with you? and if then he shall be thrust from thee by the sword, and thou be dragged to prison, and thine enemies prowl around thee like wolves for the blood of the lamb;" (D&C 122:6)

This example gets very, very personal. Instead of simply generic situations that might cause stress, the Lord sets forth an example that is heartbreaking to read. Can you imagine being falsely accused, illegally arrested, being threatened by the sword and torn from your spouse's embrace? Then your young son rushes forward, hugs you, and in terrified innocence asks what is going to happen to you? You are unable to provide comfort as your beautiful child is pushed away by a ruffian with a drawn sword, while you are hauled to a dungeon with no hope of escape. The feelings of stress and anxiety start to multiply greatly. Yet it gets even worse:

"And if thou shouldst be cast into the pit, or into the hands of murderers, and the sentence of death passed upon thee; if thou be cast into the deep; if the billowing surge conspire against thee; if fierce winds become thine enemy; if the heavens gather blackness, and all the elements combine to hedge up the way; and above all, if the very jaws of hell shall gape open the mouth wide after thee..." (D&C 122:7)

The stakes get higher and higher. No more is it simply an unfair incarceration; now we're talking about certain death. If it wasn't bad enough to have evil men plotting your demise, now the weather gets involved. The sea, winds, atmosphere, and anything else you can imagine join forces to prevent your forward movement. This is not random; heaven and earth have combined to bring you down. Then to escalate this situation to the absolute worst possible scenario, the evil maw of hell opens to consume you, consigning you to eternal suffering and damnation. I truly cannot imagine a worse outcome. It makes "perils among false brethren" seem like a walk in the park. So, what does this do to feelings of anxiety? Surely, they are through the roof at this point. It would be the same for any person I know. We have reached the maximum potential negative outcome. Anxiety, stress, and despair are the only logical emotional experiences. Yet the Lord has two more essential, clarifying points to make:

"Know thou, my son, that all these things shall give thee experience, and shall be for thy good." (D&C 122:7)

So, in other words, robbers, pits, drawn swords, panicked children, murderous thugs, evil windstorms, and the gaping jaws of hell...all of these things will be for our good and will provide essential life experience. I think I'd have a hard time believing that if the statement hadn't come from God Himself. Frankly, sometimes I still have a hard time believing it even when I know the source. But this isn't all; there is one more gem of wisdom that provides amazing perspective:

"The Son of Man hath descended below them all. Art thou greater than he?" (D&C 122:8)

For me, this is one of the most powerful verses in all of scripture. No matter how bad things get, no matter how many trials come my way, no matter how many thugs or winds or jaws threaten my very existence, it is still *nothing* compared to the sufferings experienced by our magnificent Savior. Our stress, anxiety and despair don't even move the needle when likened to the crushing weight that caused a God to bleed from every pore. Still, it doesn't seem like the Lord is trying to discount our feelings; He is not like that. He is perfectly empathetic and weeps with us. He knows our sufferings can seem very great to us in the moment. But it does appear He is trying to help us gain perspective. Even our greatest griefs are still small by certain comparisons. As we try to understand this, we can 1) see our obstacles as manageable and 2) see beyond our own self-centered views. And because He loves us, the Lord provides one more gift of hope in the final counsel to Joseph:

"Therefore, hold on thy way, and the priesthood shall remain with thee; for their bounds are set, they cannot pass. Thy days are known, and thy years shall not be numbered less; therefore, fear not what man can do, for God shall be with you forever and ever." (D&C 122:9)

Surely this counsel was specific to Joseph, yet I believe it can be applied to all (see 1 Nephi 19:23). The antidote to Joseph's stress and anxiety is provided; it is the antidote for anyone who experiences such feelings. "Fear not what man can do, for God shall be with you forever and ever." What a comforting statement! What power do winds and thugs and jaws have against their very Creator? All those things that combine to hedge up the way will retreat when commanded by their Master. As we walk hand in hand with Jesus Christ, all trials will eventually fade, and we will be made glorious. The word gospel means "good news;" can you imagine any better news that what you just read in verse nine? Those who truly come to believe and adopt that counsel will find significant relief to anxiety and stress in their lives. Their trials will not necessarily cease, but their ability to manage trials and find peace amidst the storm will increase dramatically.

You can practice the same process, by creating a list of things that tend to cause stress and anxiety in your life. For each item, answer the following questions: *Why does this cause anxiety to me? What can I do about it? What do the scriptures teach about such situations?* Here is a brief example:

Stressful event: Sometimes my children make poor decisions. This stresses me out.

Question 1: *Why does this cause anxiety to me?* I worry my children will suffer. I worry people will think I am a bad parent. I worry when I feel like I have no control over a situation.

Question 2: *What can I do about it?* In reality, I cannot force my children to do anything. Even if I could, it is not in harmony with God's plan. I want them to choose well due to their own internal motivations, not mine. So, I can be a good example to them. I can teach them correct principles. I can model good decisions. I can keep my covenants and trust that God will do His part as well. I can have faith that He loves my children even more than I do and is completely invested in their successful outcome.

Question 3: *What do the scriptures teach about such situations?* They teach that my children are free to choose their own courses in life (see 2 Nephi 2:27). They teach that parents are responsible to teach their children the gospel basics (see D&C 68:25). They teach that God is in control and He will do what is best for those who keep His commandments (see D&C 101:16).

As noted in previous chapters, you'll use a similar process of replacing less accurate thinking with a more accurate understanding of your situation. In most cases, anxiety thrives on inaccurate, inflated, exaggerated thoughts that are only loosely based in reality. Once those thoughts can be corrected, we tend to experience more reasonable emotions. Sometimes the resulting emotions still have a component of anxiety, but they are usually more manageable. For example, having gone through the previous exercise regarding anxiety of raising children, a parent may still experience fear and worry about how their children are going to turn out. However, it should be a reasonable fear, tempered with feelings of faith. Faith and fear are opposites; as one grows the other shrinks. Part of our eternal progression is to increase faith and decrease fear. This process will extend throughout our lives. It's okay to have faith and fear at the same time, but we should always try to build our faith and confront our fear. I am reminded of the man who brought his son to be healed by the Savior. The Lord questioned whether the man believed in the Savior's power to do this. The man's response was honest and wonderful: "Lord, I believe; help thou mine unbelief" (Mark 9:24). As you analyze your fears, question your doubts, and understand doctrine, you will develop an increased perspective that will help reduce feelings of anxiety and increase feelings of faith.

Understand how perfectionism is not healthy

Perfectionism is the belief that a situation or circumstance has to be "just right" or "perfect" in order to be acceptable. Since most things in life are flawed to one degree or another, perfectionists spend countless hours trying to eliminate that last, final flaw. This leads to stress, anxiety, exhaustion, and often eventual defeat as some flaws tend to persist. Consider some examples of perfectionist versus non-perfectionist thinking:

You get in an automobile accident in your new car; it is minor but leaves a two-inch scratch on the bumper.

Non-perfectionist thinking: I'm fortunate there was not more damage! My car still looks brand new. You can barely even notice the scratch.

Perfectionist thinking: My new car is trashed. It looks hideous. I might as well dump it in the scrapheap than drive around in this damaged piece of junk.

Your son comes home with his report card; he receives all A's and one A-.

Non-perfectionist thinking: My son did a great job this semester! His hard work deserves recognition. I'm grateful he is trying to do so well academically.

Perfectionist thinking: His 4.0 goal is ruined. His chances for success are dashed. He will never be able to get into a good college with these terrible grades.

Can you see how the perfectionist thinking is more likely to lead to stress and anxiety? Conversely, can you see how the non-perfectionist thinking tends to lead to feelings of peace and acceptance? Nevertheless, perfectionism is prevalent, particularly among Latter-day Saints. Many believe the deception that unless they do things "just right" they are somehow unacceptable. This may stem from an inaccurate understanding of the commandment Jesus gave during the Sermon on the Mount: "Be ye therefore perfect, even as your Father in Heaven is perfect" (Matthew 5:48). I suppose that seems pretty clear; we are to strive to be perfect like our Heavenly Father. However, this scripture does not indicate *how* or *when* we are to achieve this perfection. Other prophets have clarified this.

Moroni taught as follows: "Yea, come unto Christ, and be perfected in him, and deny yourselves of all ungodliness; and if ye shall deny yourselves of all ungodliness, and love God with all your might, mind and strength, then is his grace sufficient for you, that by his grace ye may be perfect in Christ; and if by the grace of God ye are perfect in Christ, ye can in nowise deny the power of God" (Moroni 10:32). This addresses the question of "how" we are to become perfect. Moroni makes it clear that perfection does not come through our own efforts, but only upon partnering with Christ. It is in Christ that we receive sanctification and holiness, eventually leading to godly perfection. We are to keep the commandments and love and serve God. In return, we receive the grace of the Savior which then makes us perfect. Believing we can or should become perfect without the Savior's assistance is a falsehood and deception of the adversary.

In addition, Elder Jeffrey R. Holland gave this encouragement: "May we refuse to let our own mortal follies, and the inevitable short-comings of even the best men and women around us, make us cynical about the truths of the gospel, the truthfulness of the Church, our hope for our future, or the possibility of godliness. If we persevere, then somewhere in eternity our refinement will be finished and complete—which is the New Testament meaning of *perfection*." [12] He addresses the question of "when" we are to become perfect. "Somewhere in eternity" certainly doesn't mean "right here, right now." It suggests we have time to work on this. This concept provides hope when we make mistakes and reassurance when we feel like we do not measure up. The Lord

12 Jeffrey R. Holland, "Be Ye Therefore Perfect--Eventually," *Ensign*, November 2017, 42.

expects us to do our best, make amends for our shortcomings, and trust in His process. He does not expect us to be perfect today or to beat ourselves up for falling short.

Although we are commanded to be perfect, we are not expected to do it in this life, and we are not expected to do it on our own. Those who struggle with perfectionism tend to believe the opposite. They usually believe they have to be perfect now and they have to do it with their own efforts alone. In my experience, the biggest problem with perfectionism is that *nothing is ever perfect.* There is always some flaw, ever so slight, that can be found through a diligent search. Non-perfectionists will look at a situation and be very happy for the 95% of it that is in order. Perfectionists will look at the same situation and become frustrated over the 5% that is not just right. It is a frustrating way to live because although a perfectionist demands perfection, it is never truly attained in this life. To the perfectionist, each day is just another failure and creates greater discouragement. This is contrary to the peaceable feelings the Lord wants us to experience.

One key to reducing perfectionism, and therefore reducing stress and anxiety, is to understand the difference between *unacceptable* and *undesirable* outcomes. An *unacceptable* outcome is something that under no circumstances should come to pass. It represents possible futures that we cannot accept. As a result, we work tirelessly to prevent these situations from happening. An *undesirable* outcome is something that we would prefer not to happen, but if it does happen, we will learn to accept and deal with it. Let me provide an example from my own life.

Many years ago, one of our sons entered the mission field. Unbeknownst to us, he had a fairly significant history of anxiety. While in the MTC, he started to struggle with anxiety more and more as the pressures of missionary training mounted. About four weeks into his stay he called home at the suggestion of his counselor. He told us about the anxiety but reassured us he would not be coming home. Of course, when we got that call, the first thing that ran through my mind was the high potential that he might come home. Missionaries don't call home from the MTC under normal circumstances. I knew his situation must have been a little worse than he was letting on. I considered the possibility of him coming home. To me, it was an *unacceptable* outcome. In retrospect, I was much more worried about how his return home would affect me rather than him. I worried about how it might look to others. I worried about how it would affect our family dynamic. Feelings of anxiety increased as I thought about this potential future. About four weeks later, we received another phone call from the MTC. This time we were instructed to fly to Salt Lake City immediately and bring our son home.

Because this unacceptable outcome was looking more and more likely, my feelings of anxiety spiked. *This cannot happen,* I thought. *I've got to find a way to convince the MTC to let him stay.* I considered many different arguments on the flight to Utah. I was ready to present them. I prayed fervently to have the Lord intervene and allow our son to stay on his mission. Those hours were filled with stress and anxiety. Yet when all was said and done, the three of us were on a plane, headed back to Washington. Over the year that followed, we learned to deal with the challenges and became much stronger than we would have ever been without this experience.

A number of years later, we had another son on a mission. He was also struggling. I received an unexpected call from him one Sunday morning. He explained how he was not doing well, was not enjoying mission service, and had made the decision to return home. My heart sank. I encouraged him to hang on and discuss the situation with his mission president. Yet my stress and anxiety were not as high as with my first experience of this sort. Whereas I had considered the first such experience an *unacceptable* outcome, I viewed the following experience as an *undesirable* outcome. Here was my reasoning: *I don't want my son to return home from his mission early. But if he does, we can handle it. We've been through this before and can do it again. I won't relish the chance to have another experience like this, but I know that with the Lord's help we can get through it just like we did before.* Because the outcome was no longer unacceptable, but simply undesirable, I had greater peace and confidence in the moment. These feelings helped prepare me for whatever the outcome would be.

Here are additional examples of potential outcomes, viewed through "unacceptable" and "undesirable" lenses:

Thinking that reflects "unacceptable" outcomes:

My daughter *has* to get accepted to [insert competitive university here]. If she doesn't, her college education and future preparation will be compromised. I can't believe she has a B in history right now. I've got to talk to her right away and have her improve that grade before it is too late.

My son *has* to get married in the temple. He knows what we've taught him. I can't believe he isn't following our expectations. I've got to get involved and help him think more clearly about this, so he can get back on the right path.

Thinking that reflects "undesirable" outcomes:

I would really like my daughter to get accepted to [insert competitive university here]. If she doesn't, then we'll deal with it. There will be options for future applications. Perhaps she can go to a junior college and then apply as a transfer student. I just want her to do her best and we'll work out the details from there.

It would mean the world to me for my son to marry in the temple. If he doesn't, then we'll continue to love and support him. We've taught him correctly and been good examples. I have faith that the Lord will reach out to him and help him learn from his choices and try to do what's right.

Can you see the difference between these two styles of thinking, especially as it relates to emotional outcomes? The first style of thinking leads to feelings of frustration, stress and worry. The second style of thinking leads to feelings of acceptance, calm and faith. Perfectionists often perceive certain outcomes as unacceptable. Anything that is less than perfect is usually unacceptable to them. But what if anything that is less than perfect is simply undesirable, instead of unacceptable? We still strive for excellence, but if stellar outcomes elude us, we can ultimately feel good about what we've done.

Quite frankly, perfectionism tends to deny the mercies of the Atonement of Jesus Christ. It is a deception of the adversary. Like so many of his deceptions, it leads us away from the truth. The truth is Jesus Christ died so we *can* make mistakes. Making mistakes is essential to our eternal growth. We generally learn far more from our mistakes than we do from doing something perfectly the first time.

Think about some of the situations in your life where you hold strong opinions about the way things should eventually turn out. These will be future situations; they will often relate to important things like relationships, education, career, and family. Try to think about something where for you, the outcome is non-negotiable. Then apply the following questions to your specific circumstance:

Why is this potential outcome so important to me?
Why do I feel like anything but this certain outcome will be unacceptable?
What will really happen if things don't work out the way I want them to?
If things don't go my way, what will the Lord do to continue to support me?

Answering these questions honestly will provide additional insight and potential comfort. I believe most everyone can come to the conclusion that because of the Atonement of Jesus Christ, no mortal outcome is truly unacceptable. There are many that are undesirable, but because of repentance all can be made right again. We make more room for the Savior in our lives as we stop believing that we can or have to do things perfectly and on our own. We will experience greater peace about the future. We will increase our ability to cope with trials and difficulties. Feelings of being unworthy, incomplete or unacceptable will give way to the loving embrace of the Lord. As President Boyd K. Packer taught, "Those who listen to and heed His words and the words of His chosen servants will find peace and understanding even in the midst of great heartache and sorrow. The result of His sacrifice is to free us from the effects of sin, that all may have guilt erased and feel hope." [13]

Practical suggestions for change:

Begin to see trials as growth opportunities.

Understand how the Atonement of Jesus Christ means you simply have to do your best, and failures are part of the plan.

Distinguish between unacceptable and undesirable outcomes.

---

13 Boyd K. Packer, "The Reason for Our Hope," *Ensign,* November 2014, 7.

CHAPTER NINE

How Increasing Feelings of Love Decreases Feelings of Anxiety

"For God hath not given us the spirit of fear; but of power, and of love, and of a sound mind." (2 Timothy 1:7)

We know that our main goal in this life is to transform ourselves from fallen creatures to holy beings through the power of the Atonement of Jesus Christ. While we typically associate this transformation with overcoming temptation and sin, that is not enough. We need to rid ourselves of any characteristic which is not godlike in order to become like Him.

Consider the characteristic of impatience as an example. Is it "sinful" to be impatient? I'm not certain. I don't think I need to surrender my temple recommend to the bishop if I show impatience with my spouse or children. Yet we know that our Father in Heaven is not impatient. Patience is one of His wonderful qualities, thank goodness. As we struggle over and over and over again to become better, He constantly welcomes us back. So, if we are to become like Heavenly Father, we need to develop patience. That is part of the transformation from our current mortal state to the full measure of our noble creation. Through consistent efforts, the gospel and Atonement of Jesus Christ provide the means whereby impatient people can become patient. This process can be followed with any worldly trait that is incompatible with the character of God.

I believe this also applies to anxiety. Anxiety is a terrestrial flaw that affects mortals. It is based on fear, and we know that fear is the opposite of faith. The two cannot exist in the same space; the more fear you have, the less faith; the more faith you have, the less fear. For most people, the relative balance of these two characteristics is regularly shifting. Hopefully, over time we move towards a larger balance of faith and less fear. But in order to become like our Heavenly Father, we need to eliminate fear and anxiety. Like all processes of character development, this will happen over time and with consistent effort. The process may not even be fully completed in this life but may extend into the next. Nevertheless, we need to exert efforts now in order to build celestial character and spiritual strength.

I have heard the argument that upon arriving in the afterlife, if we have been obedient, all negative characteristics will simply be swept away, and we will be transformed into godlike creatures. I do not believe this is true, my opinion being based on multiple evidences in scripture. Here are a couple such evidences that shed light on this issue.

We've previously discussed the conversion of Alma the younger. To review, Alma the younger was a very wicked person in his youth. He was the son of the prophet yet went about trying to destroy the work of his father. After much faith and many prayers from his father and others who loved him, Alma was called to repentance in dramatic fashion. An angel, speaking with the voice of thunder, commanded Alma to cease his destructive ways. The experience was massively overwhelming to Alma, such that he fell unconscious for three days. On the third day he awoke, having had a mighty spiritual experience during his unconsciousness. He told his father, "I have repented of my sins, and have been redeemed of the Lord; behold I am born of the Spirit.... after wading through much tribulation, repenting nigh unto death, the Lord in mercy hath seen fit to snatch me out of an everlasting burning, and I am born of God.... I was in the darkest abyss; but now I behold the marvelous light of God. My soul was racked with eternal torment; but I am snatched, and my soul is pained no more" (Mosiah 27:24, 28-29).

As a youth I used to think, "Man, that would be pretty cool. To be able to get over all your problems in just three days!" In some ways I envied Alma and was bitter about my own process of change. Why was I consigned to have to work out my salvation day after day, month after month, and year after year, slowly plugging away, when apparently there was a "three-day" option available? I felt a little cheated. However, as I grew older and wiser, I realized that there is no three-day option.

In later years, Alma described his conversion to his son Helaman. He discussed being "racked with torment" during those three days, being stunned with the weight of his sinful behavior. Even if there was a three-day option, it sounded less and less appealing as Alma detailed the process. Then he made a significant statement to his son, which altered my thinking about how we all change: "Yea, and from that time even until now, *I have labored without ceasing*, that I might bring souls unto repentance; that I might bring them to taste of the exceeding joy of which I did taste; that they might also be born of God, and be filled with the Holy Ghost" (Alma 36:24, emphasis added).

"I have labored without ceasing." While the three days of torment were perhaps the catalyst for his change, the true measure of Alma's conversion was his subsequent behavior. Three days would not make much difference to anyone, regardless of the magnitude of the spiritual event, if not followed by three hundred or three thousand days of consistent, obedient behavior. The Book of Mormon is filled with dozens of examples of individuals and groups who had significant spiritual experiences, yet shortly thereafter returned to prior sinful ways. Dramatic experiences can produce forks in the road of life's journey, but taking the covenant path and staying on it for years and years is what produces lasting change. Thus, Alma's negative characteristics of disobedience and rebellion were *not* simply swept away. They changed, over time, as the result of consistent obedience.

Amulek taught doctrine which provides additional evidence that suggests negative characteristics do not magically vanish upon our exit from this life. He taught, "For behold, this life is the time for men to prepare to meet God; yea, behold the day of this life is the day for men to perform their labors" (Alma 34:32). Most of us know this. We know we are here to improve ourselves. However, what is left undone in life is apparently left undone in the afterlife as well. Amulek continues, "That same spirit which doth possess your bodies at the time that ye go out of this life, that same spirit will have power to possess your body in that eternal world" (Alma 34:34). This does not suggest that change is not possible after this life. We know that it is possible because the gospel is preached to the dead. We do vicarious saving ordinances in holy temples. But Amulek's teachings do suggest that if I struggle with issues in this life, I will struggle with the same issues in the next life. I believe I will continue to work out my salvation in largely the same way I do in mortality: one choice at a time.

What does this have to do with anxiety management? It goes back to concepts we have discussed previously. Some say, "I'm just an anxious person. It's part of my character. There's nothing I can do about it." True, some people have anxiety issues that appear to be present from birth. They could very well be part of their personality structure. *But that does not mean these issues cannot or should not be changed.* Remember, God does not have anxiety. It is contrary to His very nature. If we are going to become like God, we have to eliminate anxiety from our lives as well. Is there a "three-day" option for this? I'm afraid not. Do we have to completely eradicate anxiety from our personalities while in this life? I don't believe so. But we do have to provide our best efforts, working hard, making daily choices that will help us go from fear to faith. We have to rely on the mercies of the Savior and follow His commandments and example.

Having had personal experience with anxiety management, I am familiar with the overwhelming magnitude of this proposed task. Then one day I read a scripture that astonished me. It is in the Book of Mormon, from a letter written by Mormon to his son Moroni. The same doctrine is also included in the New Testament in the writings of John the Beloved. Mormon wrote, "Behold, I speak with boldness, having authority from God; and I fear not what man can do; for perfect love casteth out all fear" (Moroni 8:16). This truly caught my attention. "Perfect love casteth out all fear." *All fear?* Like every last bit of fear? In some ways this seemed too good to be true. It was a promise from a prophet, with a simple tutorial of how to eliminate anxiety and fear. It sounded great to me, as I don't like feeling anxious. I would love to have a life filled with faith, where fears are eliminated.

But Mormon's counsel was still puzzling to me. If he had written "perfect *faith* casteth out all fear," that would have made much more sense to me. As we have already discussed, faith and fear are opposites. It makes sense that the increase of one facilitates the decrease of the other. Therefore, perfect faith would truly eliminate all fear. But perfect love? What does an increase in love have to do with a decrease in fear? I have thought about this for many years and believe I have some helpful insights.

Jesus Christ distilled *all* commandments down to two crucial directives: "Thou shalt love the Lord thy God with all thy heart, and with all thy soul, and with all thy mind. This is the first and great commandment. And the second is like unto it, Thou shalt love thy neighbour as thyself. On these two commandments hang all the law and the prophets" (Matthew 22:37-40). How are we to show love for God? Jesus answered that as well: "If ye love me, keep my commandments" (John 14:15). Yet what about loving our neighbor? The Savior also gave multiple examples of how to do this. Consider the parable of the Good Samaritan. Where the priest and Levite did not stop to help the wounded traveler, the outcast Samaritan went above and beyond to help this person who likely saw him as an enemy. The love he showed for his neighbor transcended geography, politics, and personal affronts. It was a deep and abiding love for the welfare of this man. This is the standard set by the Savior as we are commanded to love our neighbor.

But the commandment is not simply to love our neighbor. It is to love our neighbor *as ourselves.* That means we should show the same love and concern for our neighbor as we do for our own selves. This raises an interesting question. What if someone does not love themselves? What if they have terrible self-esteem? What if they look in the mirror each morning and think, "I'm a horrible person. No one would love me. I'm a waste of space on this earth." On a scale of 0 to 100, that person's love for self would probably be close to zero. Does that mean they can love their neighbor with a "zero" effort? Would that be consistent with the commandment? "Today I treated my neighbor like garbage, because I feel like garbage myself; therefore I'm in compliance with the second great commandment." That does not seem right to me.

We know the standard the Lord has set for love of others. I believe this also infers the standard the Lord has set for how we should love ourselves. If love of others requires patience with their shortcomings, forgiveness of their transgressions, tending to their needs and lifting them when downtrodden, shouldn't we apply the same standard to ourselves? The apostle John recorded, "If a man say, I love God, and hateth his brother, he is a liar" (1 John 4:20). Now, I'm not going to go so far to declare if a person says "I love my brother but I hate myself" they are a liar, but I will say that if we hate ourselves, we have compromised our ability to truly love others. A healthy love of self is essential in spiritual development and in learning how to love our fellow man as God has commanded.

I worked with a man who had very low self-esteem. His confidence had been battered for years because of the thoughtless behavior of those who should have loved and supported him. We talked about how he needed to think more accurately and positively about himself. He took the blame for everything wrong in his life, even if it wasn't remotely his fault. Yet when he was able to accomplish something good, he made statements such as, "Well, it was really easy," or "I didn't have that much to do with it." Those statements were untrue as he genuinely had done something good through his own choices and efforts. As we discussed what could be done in order to have him show greater love for himself, he said, "I don't want to work too hard at this, because I don't want to get a big head. I don't want to swing to the other side and become some raging egomaniac." I assured him that he was so far in the other direction, that if he gave all of his effort to move towards greater self-confidence, he would barely arrive in the middle of the spectrum. I did not see "raging egomaniac" as a possible future for him. This man did not love himself. He did not see himself as God sees him. His confidence was extremely low.

This man had symptoms of depression, consequent to his abusive history and poor self-concept. I fully expected such symptoms given his overall situation. What is interesting is he had symptoms of anxiety as well. He was worried about the opinions of others, he became paralyzed by even simple decisions, and he constantly doubted his choices. I was not expecting to see symptoms of anxiety, but after greater consideration of his situation, it became clear. He did not believe in himself. He did not believe in his abilities. He thought everything he did would turn out wrong. In addition to creating depression symptoms, these experiences also contributed to feelings of stress, worry, and anxiety.

It was then I began to see the truth in Mormon's statement, "perfect love casteth out all fear" (Moroni 8:16). The relationship between love and fear became clearer. "Perfect love" is God's love. It is to love people as God loves them. Truly He follows His own commandments. He loves His neighbor as Himself. We have ample evidence of how He loves His neighbor, who are His children. He treats us with gentle kindness and showers us with everlasting compassion and grace. As our capacity for love approaches the "perfect love" that God has, we will love our neighbor with greater depth. I also believe that as we more effectively learn to love God and our neighbor, our love for ourselves will become refined and healthy. There will be fewer inconsistencies between our love for others and love for ourselves. We will see them as God sees them: children of heavenly parents who are worthy of compassion and concern. We will also start to see ourselves as God sees us: His children who are worthy of compassion and concern.

There are still many who do not believe God loves them. Although they believe He has a certain obligation to love them as a responsible parent, they do not believe they are always worthy of His love. They reason that through their behaviors, they fall short and are therefore outside of His good graces. The fellow I referred to earlier in this chapter felt like that all the time. He would say, "I know God loves His children, but I don't think He loves me all the time. How could He? Look at the things I've done. Look at all the mistakes I've made. Look at how I come back to Him over and over again with the same problems; surely He has grown weary of me and His love has grown cold." If you have ever had similar thoughts and feelings, let me assure you as I assured this man. *Heavenly Father loves you.* I don't care what you've done, where you've been, or how you've treated Him in the past. *He loves you.* He will love you forever. You are His child and He will always acknowledge and cherish that relationship. The belief that we can sin our way out of God's love is false and a pure deception of Satan.

Elder Jeffrey R. Holland made this point very eloquently: "However late you think you are, however many chances you think you have missed, however many mistakes you feel you have made or talents you think you don't have, or however far from home and family and God you feel you have traveled, I testify that you have *not* traveled beyond the reach of divine love. It is not possible for you to sink lower than the infinite light of Christ's Atonement shines." [14] This is absolutely true. The Atonement of Jesus Christ is sufficient for all who come to Him with full purpose of heart. Love was the primary motivation for the Savior's sacrifice. That love endures today and will endure forever. It is a love for us.

Accurately understanding God's love for you will help you develop greater love for yourself. Here are some scriptures that help us understand the nature and depth of God's love for each of His children.

"O ye house of Israel whom I have spared, how oft will I gather you as a hen gathereth her chickens under her wings, if ye will repent and return unto me with full purpose of heart." (3 Nephi 10:6)

These are the words of the Lord to the American saints between His death and resurrection. There were terrible destructions upon the land and many perished. Those who survived heard the voice of God. This scripture characterizes the Lord's willingness to ever forgive and accept us. The conditions are clear; we must return to Him with integrity and full desire. He will always accept those who do. He who admonished us to forgive "until seventy times seven" (Matthew 18:22) will receive and forgive us time and time again, because He loves us.

"When Jesus had lifted up himself, and saw none but the woman, he said unto her, Woman, where are those thine accusers? hath no man condemned thee? She said, No man, Lord. And Jesus said unto her, neither do I condemn thee: go, and sin no more." (John 8:10-11)

Many will recall the story of the woman taken in adultery. Callous and self-righteous men dragged her to the Savior, demanding of Him to either look the other way on such a serious sin, or sentence her to death as indicated in the law. The Master easily deflected their temptation, suggesting he who had no sin throw the first stone. As they each slunk away, ashamed and chagrined, the Savior was left alone with the sinful woman. He commanded her to not sin again, but there was no condemnation. There was no "I can't believe you did this! Don't you know better? Adultery is an extremely serious sin; what were you thinking?" His love and acceptance of the woman was complete *despite* her sinful ways. Sin does not make us unlovable before God. On the

---

14 Jeffrey R. Holland, "The Laborers in the Vineyard," *Ensign,* May 2012, 22.

contrary, the Good Shepherd leaves the ninety and nine to go after the one that is lost.

"We love him, because he first loved us." (1 John 4:19)

It seems like it is much easier to love someone who first shows love to us. We tend to be afraid of rejection and don't want to be the first one to say, "I love you," for fear that the feeling will not be reciprocated. However, we never need to fear this when it comes to our Father in Heaven. He loved us first. He has always loved us.

"Greater love hath no man than this, that a man lay down his life for his friends." (John 15:13)

Jesus spoke these words at the last supper, only hours before He would literally demonstrate the principle He taught. Perhaps the greatest evidence of the Savior's love for all of us is the fact that He willingly suffered and died on our behalf. What is most interesting is that the Atonement of Jesus Christ is not limited to those who are likely to repent. It is available to all, whether they will repent or not. Jesus paid the price for those sinners who were doubtful to ever repent. Perhaps He already knew, with godly foreknowledge, who were likely to come to Him and who were not. Nevertheless, He paid for *all* sins, for *all* people, so His gift could be complete. The magnitude and comprehensive nature of His sacrifice is clear evidence of His love for each of us.

"For God so loved the world, that he gave his only begotten Son, that whosoever believeth in him should not perish, but have everlasting life." (John 3:16)

Finally, the love of our Father in Heaven is dramatically manifest in the gift of his one perfect Son. I cannot imagine the grief, standing idly by while watching your only truly obedient son being brutalized by his spiritually-blinded siblings. Truly God the Father could have sent "more than twelve legions of angels" (Matthew 26:53) to save his Son from cruel torture and pain. Yet He resisted. He resisted for us. He knew that saving his well-beloved Son from grief and suffering would ensure an eternity of pain and misery for the rest of His children. If you ever doubt God's love for you, take some time to read the New Testament account of the suffering in the garden of Gethsemane. Study the vicious treatment prior to crucifixion and the unfathomable torture of being nailed to a cross. Consider how each second of those nine excruciating hours probably seemed like an eternity. I promise you will gain a much greater appreciation of how much your Father in Heaven loves you as you realize how much He sacrificed to save you.

Increasing love of self will increase self-confidence. Increasing self-confidence will decrease fear and anxiety. I believe it is that simple. I'm not suggesting this should be the only front you fight in your battle against anxiety. I *am* suggesting you add this to the many strategies you use to overcome anxiety in general. As you confront negative beliefs, practice meditation, try to visualize positive outcomes, and deepen your understanding of the Atonement of Jesus Christ, add "increase love of self" to the list of tools you can use to decrease anxiety.

Practical suggestions for change:

Prayerfully seek to understand and feel the depth of God's individual and personal love for you.

Seek to develop greater confidence in and love for yourself, using the love of God as a benchmark and model.

CHAPTER TEN

How to Better Understand and Help Those Who Deal With Anxiety

"Yea, and are willing to mourn with those that mourn; yea, and comfort those that stand in need of comfort." (Mosiah 18:9)

This chapter is different from the previous ones, inasmuch as the intended audience is a separate group. So far, we have been talking about specific spiritual strategies and gospel concepts to help individuals manage anxiety. In this chapter we'll talk directly to those who support or otherwise help those who have anxiety issues. These could be friends, family members, ministering brothers and sisters, caregivers, professionals, and many others. If you have a friend or loved one who has had chronic struggles with anxiety, you know the frustration this can have on both the person who suffers *and* the person who supports them. I hope to provide some insight and suggestions regarding how to best help and assist those with anxiety problems. Hand your copy of this book to those friends and loved ones and have them read this chapter. To those who do not suffer from anxiety but are trying to support someone who does, please consider the following suggestions.

Tip #1: You are not responsible for changes in others

I had to get practical experience in my training to become a psychologist. Part of this involved working with a community agency, with *real* clients. Up until then we had practiced counseling techniques on our fellow students but never in a real setting. I remember one client in particular. She was in her mid-twenties, a single mother, and had many emotional problems. Most of these stemmed from a toxic relationship she had with her mother. Her mother's support had varied wildly throughout the years. I'm not even sure I would call it "support";

it could be better characterized as the mother having emotionally manipulated the daughter for decades. This took a toll on the daughter, and she was not emotionally grounded. As a result, she experienced depression, anxiety, stress and behavioral instability.

As a *very* inexperienced counselor, I tried my best to help her. I remember coming up with what I thought were good ideas. These ideas were designed to help her improve her relationship with her mother. Each time I proposed an idea, my client immediately shot it down. I'd go back to the drawing board and come up with a better, more refined solution. I'd bring it up, she'd pull out her "idea shotgun" and blast my idea to smithereens. This process repeated over and over. I found myself getting very tired. I was running out of ideas. Then I noticed something interesting. My client didn't seem as tired as I was. She didn't seem as distressed as I was. In fact, in some ways she seemed to enjoy this "idea target practice" we had been having. I realized I was working much, much harder than she was. The biggest issue with this was that these were not *my* problems we were working on; they were hers. It felt wrong that I was working harder to solve her concerns than she was.

With time and additional training, I was able to learn better techniques and professional boundaries. I also learned a very important lesson. *I was not personally responsible for another's choice to change.* I could encourage, instruct, motivate, educate, model, and support, but if they chose not to change, that was their decision and not mine. Try to remember this as you support friends who have anxiety issues. Your efforts will not guarantee certain outcomes in their lives. You have not failed if they continue to experience symptoms. Do your best but recognize and accept that your assistance will have limited utility at times.

Tip #2: You cannot force people to make choices

Most people will read this tip and say, "That's a no-brainer. Everyone knows you can't force people to do things." I'm not as convinced that everyone knows this. I do believe some people realize they cannot force others. However, there are still very many out there who feel they can subtly manipulate other people to eventually do what they want. This reminds me of a certain situation in the Garden of

Eden. Eve had received a commandment to not partake of the fruit of the tree of knowledge of good and evil. She knew what would happen if she did partake. Lucifer approached her, encouraging her to eat the fruit. Eve rightly responded saying if she were to eat of that fruit, she would die. Lucifer's direct approach apparently failed. Yet he was not finished. "And the serpent said unto the woman: Ye shall not surely die; For God doth know that in the day ye eat thereof, then your eyes shall be opened, and ye shall be as gods, knowing good and evil" (Moses 4:10-11). Satan was eventually able to get Eve to do as he wished. But ultimately it was Eve's choice. He truly did not force her. He made a compelling argument and Eve made a reasoned decision.

When dealing with people who have anxiety, sometimes you may feel you have a much clearer understanding of their situation than they do. This is true in many cases. You may naturally feel a desire to help correct their thinking and feelings. You may want them to make different choices in certain situations. You may begin to design plans, strategies, and sophisticated approaches to help them choose in a way that you think is best. Please don't do that. There are two main reasons why you shouldn't do this. First, it doesn't work. Even though you think you might be leading someone down your well-intentioned path for their behavioral change, you really aren't. Their choices are still theirs and you cannot truly manipulate outcomes. Second, you are not helping them if you are choosing for them. Effective and lasting change happens when people make their *own* decisions based on their *own* realizations. Why do you think Heavenly Father doesn't force or manipulate us into good decisions? It's because He knows that will not lead to true conversion and discipleship. Don't try to push your good intentions on others. Let them come to their own conclusions, regardless of how long that takes or how many missteps they make in the process.

Tip #3: Know your own limits

When I was doing my psychologist residency training, I worked in an inpatient psychiatric unit. In most instances, patients were only there for a short period of time. This was often five to seven days, just long enough for them to be stabilized. On occasion, we would receive patients who had been court ordered to stay in such settings for a longer period of time. I remember one particular patient; she was on the unit for four months, which was a very long time relative to most. She was a recovering heroin addict in addition to being severely personality disordered. Essentially, she was highly manipulative, highly suicidal, and highly demanding. I was assigned as her day-to-day mental health therapist. She was extremely difficult to deal with, as each day she would test limits and be emotionally abusive.

I was still new to my career and was eager to prove to my superiors that I could handle anything that came my way. Yet with this patient, I had truly met my match. After about three months with her, I was completely burned out. I remember having a frank discussion with her where I told her I didn't like the way she had been treating me, and I was going to hand her off to another therapist. She broke into tears and said, "You're leaving me just like everyone always leaves me." She was on the unit for another few weeks until she was eventually transferred to the state hospital. Our therapy relationship was never the same. I felt badly about the outcome. After her transfer, her mother came to the hospital to thank us for having worked with her. She said something I have never forgotten: "God keeps sending angels into her life, and they are eventually carried out on stretchers."

Sometimes working with people who have chronic anxiety can be very difficult. It can test your patience. You *must* know your own limits and take adequate time for self-care. If you burn yourself out, like I did in the case I mentioned, you will not be able to be helpful any longer. There are going to be times when you have to take time for yourself. As you do this, you'll be better prepared and equipped to help others. Running yourself ragged until you run out of gas will make you a less effective helper in the long term. Give what help and support you can to others, but remember to save a portion for your own emotional sustenance.

Tip #4: There is nothing wrong with suffering if it leads to good outcomes

When Alma and Amulek preached to the people of Ammonihah, the majority rejected them. There were a few believers, but they were a small group. The non-believers were angry and vindictive, to the point that they murdered those who believed in God. The men were stoned to death. Their wives and children were taken to a flaming pit and thrown in where they burned alive. The wicked leaders brought Alma and Amulek to the pit to show them the burning women and children. It was a horrible sight. It may have felt particularly bad if Alma and Amulek believed that perhaps it was their fault that this evil event was happening. Amulek appeared especially grieved. He was only recently reactivated in the gospel and was rebuilding his faith and testimony. He pled with Alma: "How can we witness this awful scene? Therefore let us stretch forth our hands, and exercise the power of God which is in us, and save them from the flames" (Alma 14:10). Alma, having more spiritual experience and a greater sensitivity to the Spirit, responded as follows: "The Spirit constraineth me that I must not stretch forth mine hand; for behold the Lord receiveth them up unto himself, in glory" (Alma 14:11). He went on to explain that this tragic scene was being permitted by God in order to save the souls of the innocent and ensure a righteous condemnation of the guilty.

Sometimes we have a tendency to view all suffering as tragic or unacceptable. This can be particularly true when those who suffer are our children, friends, or loved ones. We feel a desire to do everything we can to help eliminate the trial and end the pain. Yet this is not always wise. It is not always in harmony with Heavenly Father's plan for us. Travail and difficulty are most certainly part of our plan of growth and sanctification. If someone you care for has anxiety, don't panic. Don't treat it like a fire that needs to be put out immediately. Try to understand how this experience will help them grow and progress. I'm not suggesting you do nothing to help either. On the contrary, this whole chapter is about what you *can* do to help those who suffer with anxiety. I'm simply suggesting you try to see beyond the immediate consequences and take a broader view of the situation. In almost every case, our trials are an essential part of our growth process.

Tip #5: Be patient

There are few things worse than working as hard as you can and still feeling like you come up short. This creates feelings of failure and frustration, as you believe you are underperforming but feel like you have nothing left to give. This is a common experience with people who suffer from anxiety. They know the expectations yet feel they cannot fulfill them, even with their best efforts. For those who are watching from a distance, it can be a frustrating experience. They often think, "Why isn't this person trying harder? It's not like they're being asked to do a truly difficult thing. Why can't they just get it together?" This type of thinking can be common but is insensitive and unhelpful.

Part of the problem is that we cannot truly understand the experiences of others with our limited vantage points. Let's say you were observing two hikers ascending a trail. One moved fairly quickly and with evident ease. The other moved slowly, took multiple breaks, and appeared to be in distress. It would be easy to surmise that the first hiker was clearly working harder and was more motivated than the second. But that is not necessarily true, as we don't know enough about the situation. Here's a little more information. The first hiker is young, healthy, and well experienced in hiking trails. This particular trail is one of the easier ones he has ever hiked. The second hiker is older, has terminal cancer, and has never hiked this trail before. He promised himself that before he died, he would hike this trail to prove to himself he could do it. For him, each step is painful and exhausting. With this new insight, which hiker appears to be working harder? The answer is clear.

When trying to support those who have anxiety, be patient with their efforts. Even though they may not look like they are moving forward very quickly, they may be doing the best they can. Encouragement and support will help them move along. Criticism and impatience will only complicate their already difficult journey.

Tip #6: Be insistent

This suggestion may seem to be the opposite of the previous suggestion, but it is helpful nonetheless. As we already discussed, those with anxiety may feel quite overwhelmed at times. They may feel as if a certain task is beyond their capacities. However, many times, they are actually capable of doing what is required and are simply frightened to do it. I remember a time when my church assignment in our ward was to ask people to give prayers to open and close sacrament meeting. This required them to pray aloud in front of about 150 people. Some members quickly agreed to pray when asked. Others were less willing, due to anxiety about public speaking. I remember one woman in particular, who was very capable but had much anxiety. I knew if I asked her to pray she would likely be very nervous about the prospect. As such, I tried to tread carefully.

One Sunday morning, the person I had asked to pray was sick and unable to attend the meeting. I thought about who I could get for a replacement. Immediately my mind went to this other woman who was anxious about public speaking. I approached her and said, "I know you don't want to, and I know it will make you nervous, but will you give the opening prayer in our meeting this morning?" She reluctantly agreed. As the moment approached, I could sense her anxiety increasing. She walked to the pulpit, gave a fine prayer, and went back to her seat. Afterwards I thanked her very much for her help. She said, "It wasn't as bad as I thought, but don't ask me again anytime soon." I smiled and agreed to consider her request.

I was well aware of her fears before I asked her to pray. Yet I was not deterred, because I knew she was perfectly able to do it. Her feelings of anxiety told her otherwise, but they created a false sense of inability. I hope this experience helped her realize what she was capable of. In many cases, you will have loved ones who do not want to do certain things due to anxiety. Even though they may not think it is helpful at first, your encouragement and periodic insistence can help them reach beyond what they think they can accomplish. Make sure you exercise good judgment in such situations. If we were to combine the suggestions in tips five and six, I'd say there are times when you need to lay off and there are times when you need to push a little. As you prayerfully consider how to best help, the Holy Ghost will guide you to know what to do and when.

Tip #7: Don't presume they can't see their own distorted thinking

Under most conditions, there is nothing dangerous or life-threatening about walking into a crowded grocery store. Yet some people react to this as if they are being chased by a mountain lion. They feel like they might actually die if they have to go in and buy a bag of Cheetos during the 5:00 p.m. shopping rush. In their mind, they see themselves walking to the chips aisle. The crowds are overflowing. Their heart pounds. As their vision blurs, they are barely able to tell the Cheetos from the Fritos. They grab the bag and rush to the checkout, crowds pressing on them with each step. As they get into a line of thirty people, children rushing about them, the elevator music seeming to blast in their ears, the anxiety peaks. Their heart literally explodes as they fall dead, the bag of chips dropping from their grip with finality. With their last breath, they think, "Why did I do that? All for a bag of Cheetos..."

I don't mean to make light of serious situations. But we all know there is nothing deadly about going into a crowded store. *People with anxiety know this too.* They know what is accurate, but their feelings create other sensations that are hard to resist at times. These sensations compete with reality and create inaccurate perceptions. You don't need to sit down with your friends and say, "The store isn't going to kill you. You are thinking irrationally." They already know that. In fact, it might just be more frustrating for them as you draw attention to their distorted thinking. This is especially true if you are exasperated or impatient. "Just get out of the car and come into the darn store already! Nothing terrible is going to happen!" This type of "encouragement" is generally not helpful and will only make matters worse.

Of course, it is absolutely true that anxiety management improves as people are able to better notice and correct their inaccurate thinking. But we should leave that to the experts. Mental health professionals are skilled in how to intervene with proper techniques and accurate timing. They know when to push and they know when to lighten up. Rather than trying to play junior therapist to your friends, encourage them to seek professional help and be there to support them through the process.

Tip #8: Listen and support without trying to fix things

When Nephi and his brothers returned to Jerusalem to seek the plates of brass, their task was daunting. The journey was long and dangerous. There was no guarantee they would be successful. If Laban didn't kill them, then they could have been killed by the thieves who marauded the wilderness. An awareness of such risks was not lost on their mother, Sariah. As her sons delayed in their return, she began to assume the worst. I can only imagine the agony of a mother who believes her sons have died. Even worse, it was due to her husband's command they left in the first place. On a particularly bad day, Sariah apparently couldn't hold back any longer and complained to her husband Lehi. She complained that he had taken them from their comfortable home in Jerusalem. She complained that because of this, her sons were now dead. She further complained that the rest of them would die in the wilderness as well. Sariah even called Lehi a "visionary man," which I don't think was meant as a compliment in the moment (see 1 Nephi 5:1-3).

Sariah's feelings were legitimate, but they were not based in rational thought. She presumed her sons were dead but had no evidence of this. She felt angry because she believed the rest of the family was going to die as well, yet in the moment they were alive and safe. She blamed Lehi as the cause of these uncertain and untrue events. Lehi could have become defensive. He could have responded in kind and blamed Sariah for being faithless and critical. Instead, he took responsibility for his decisions and bore witness to his wife of what he knew was true: "I know that I am a visionary man; for if I had not seen the things of God in a vision I should not have known the goodness of God, but had tarried at Jerusalem, and had perished with my brethren. But behold, I have obtained a land of promise, in the which things I do rejoice; yea, and I know that the Lord will deliver my sons out of the hands of Laban, and bring them down again unto us in the wilderness" (1 Nephi 5:4-5). The scriptures record that Lehi's words comforted his dear wife. When her sons returned safe, Sariah's comfort was then complete.

When you are dealing with people who have anxiety, their thoughts and perceptions are often going to be inaccurate. Trying to correct their thinking or trying to "set them straight" in the moment is not very helpful. Most often they just need a listening ear and a word of faith. Notice from Lehi's response to Sariah: he told her that he knew things were going to work out. Even though she had a hard time believing that in the moment, she was able to receive comfort from Lehi's testimony and faith in the Lord's assurances. You can do the same. You can comfort your friends by bearing witness of what you know is true. While neither of you know the end from the beginning, you can explain to them how you know the Lord loves them. You can witness how God is mindful of our situation. You can testify that not only will the Lord never give us any task we cannot handle, He will provide both the path and the strength to accomplish the task. Such faithful reassurances can be much more helpful than trying to fix what is broken.

Tip #9: Have good timing

Almost any intervention is only as good as its timing. Even the best ideas can flop if they are applied at an inopportune time. When I was working at an inpatient psychiatric hospital, we dealt with severe mental health issues. There was one young man who had been admitted after being found running naked down the highway. He was in a severe manic phase of bipolar disorder. After being brought to the unit, he was so agitated that we had to keep him in seclusion for a considerable period of time. He attacked several of the nurses who attempted to administer medication. I was the lead therapist on the unit and everyone looked to me to do something about this bad situation. I was also very young and had only barely finished my doctorate. I decided I was going to march into the seclusion room and tell this young man how it was going to be. We would not tolerate violence on the unit. He would be respectful of our nurses. If he complied with expectations, he would eventually be permitted to leave. He had to listen to me because I was Doctor Morgan. I went into the seclusion room armed with my monologue. You can probably guess what happened. He lunged to attack me as well. Doctor Morgan fled like a scared child. Some weeks later, after medication had a chance to work and his mood was more stable, we had the talk that I had planned. It was much more effective the second time.

If you have a friend or loved one who is in a full-blown panic attack, that moment is probably not the best time to help them realize the irrational nature of the beliefs that contribute to their anxiety. Think of it as putting out a fire. Say you walk into a room and see

1) your toddler son standing next to an open box of matches and 2) your living room couch on fire. There are two issues that need to be addressed. One is the fact that your son has been playing with matches. The other is the fact that the couch is on fire. Let's deal with the couch first and the son later. With anxiety issues, during moments of high stress and emotion, it's best to simply provide support and comfort. Later there will be time to talk about what caused the anxiety, what situations preceded it, and how you can help them in the future. Good interventions are based on good timing.

Tip #10: Try to empathize

Sometimes it can be difficult to understand what someone is going through. This can be particularly challenging if it is something you have never experienced. Most of the time we only have our own frame of reference to try to appreciate the feelings of others. If you are trying to support someone who has anxiety, and you have never had problems with anxiety, you may find yourself getting easily frustrated. You may wonder, "Why can't they just snap out of this? Why is this so difficult for them?" Trying to put yourself in their situation can be a good way of developing greater empathy and compassion.

Jesus Christ is the ultimate example of empathy and compassion. In some ways, it seems He would be the most unlikely candidate to understand our challenges, having lived a sinless life. Yet because of His sufferings in the garden and on the cross, He has become intimately acquainted with our weaknesses and trials. "And he shall go forth, suffering pains and afflictions and temptations of every kind; and this that the word might be fulfilled which saith he will take upon him the pains and the sicknesses of his people. And he will take upon him death, that he may loose the bands of death which bind his people; and he will take upon him their infirmities, that his bowels may be filled with mercy, according to the flesh, that he may know according to the flesh how to succor his people according to their infirmities" (Alma 7:11-12).

Many know that Jesus Christ suffered for our sins, thus enabling the process of repentance. Fewer realize he also suffered our pains, sicknesses, heartaches, losses, and every other type of emotional or physical sorrow you can conceive. Truly there is *nothing* you can experience that He has not already experienced on your behalf. In the previous scripture, Alma explains why the Savior not only bore our sins but bore our sorrows as well: so that he could be perfectly merciful and know how to help and support us during our trials. He is our ultimate example of how we should treat others who struggle with any affliction. He is not impatient. He is not condescending. He is not frustrated. He is perfectly compassionate, loving, and merciful. Surely, we have all experienced His loving kindness during moments of terrible grief. It is one of the sweetest feelings I know of.

As you try to empathize with and show compassion for your associates who struggle with anxiety, draw upon your own experiences in order to understand them better. Perhaps you have never had severe anxiety. You don't know what it's like to walk into a crowd and feel like you are having a heart attack. But have you ever felt fear? Have you ever been overwhelmed? Have you ever felt hopeless? Even though you may not have had such feelings in the context of anxiety, *they are the same emotions.* When you felt fearful, overwhelmed or hopeless, regardless of the reason, think about how you wanted to be treated. Think about what would have been helpful in such moments. You can use those experiences to develop greater understanding and thus provide more effective support to your friends and family who have problems with anxiety.

Here is a summary of the ten suggestions:

Tip #1: You are not responsible for changes in others

Tip #2: You cannot force people to make choices

Tip #3: Know your own limits

Tip #4: There is nothing wrong with suffering if it leads to good outcomes

Tip #5: Be patient

Tip #6: Be insistent

Tip #7: Don't presume they can't see their own distorted thinking

Tip #8: Listen and support without trying to fix things

Tip #9: Have good timing

Tip #10: Try to empathize

God bless you as you do your best to love and sustain those

around you. By supporting others, we fulfill the Lord's commandment to "succor the weak, lift up the hands that hang down, and strengthen the feeble knees" (D&C 81:5). It is also one of the purest forms to serve the Savior. As we help others in their weakness and moments of trouble, we are truly serving Him. "And the King shall answer and say unto them, Verily I say unto you, Inasmuch as ye have done it unto one of the least of these my brethren, ye have done it unto me" (Matthew 25:40).

Practical suggestions for change:

Develop a greater understanding of the Savior's love for you and then use that as a model to love and support others.

Reflect on your own challenges and use these experiences to develop greater empathy for those around you.

CHAPTER ELEVEN
Confidence is Key to Change

"Be of good courage, and he shall strengthen your heart, all ye that hope in the Lord." (Psalm 31:24)

Henry Ford is attributed to having said, "Whether you believe you can do a thing or not, you are right." [15] I think that is true. So much of our success or failure in life depends upon our attitude. My primary intention in writing this book is to give people hope. I want those who feel trapped to see a way out. I want those who feel disheartened to increase their confidence. Confidence comes from moving forward in faith. Consider the relative roles of God and man in the following scripture: "Draw near unto me and I will draw near unto you; seek me diligently and ye shall find me; ask, and ye shall receive; knock, and it shall be opened unto you" (D&C 88:63). There are wonderful promises in this verse. Yet each one of them begins with action on our part. *Moving closer* to the Lord results in Him moving closer to you. *Seeking* Him results in you finding Him. *Asking* results in receiving; *knocking* generates open doors. In each case, the Lord expects us to do our part first. He is ever willing, and actually obligated, to bless us when we first do as He has asked (see D&C 82:10). But we must commit to action first. We must take the first step, which is then followed by the Lord fulfilling His promises. *We have to start the process.*

The prophet Abinadi preached the word of God to a very wicked people. They did not change their ways. In fact, they burned him alive. Unbeknownst to Abinadi at the time, he had one single convert. Alma the Elder, who was a wicked priest of King Noah, believed Abinadi's words. Alma was cast out because of his beliefs. He spent time writing

15 Henry Ford, *The Reader's Digest*, The Reader's Digest Association, Volume 51, Page 64, 1947. https://quoteinvestigator.com/2015/02/03/you-can/.

down what Abinadi said and then started a church. He baptized the believers and they studied and lived the word of God. These people had repented, changed their ways, and were walking on the covenant path. The Lord had truly blessed them for their obedience. Then tragedy struck. Out of nowhere, a Lamanite army discovered their remote city. These hostile Lamanites gathered and started to approach the people. The people were terrified. I can imagine this would be like you sitting at home, reading a book, and then a SWAT team shows up. Dozens of armed officers point guns at your windows. Your anxiety goes through the roof. That was the experience of Alma's people as well. They quickly left their homes, probably gathered their families, and went to the city center with Alma. Perhaps the following thoughts raced through their minds: "What will happen to us? We are defenseless against such a powerful army. The Lamanites hate us and are known killers. We are dead for sure." If they had such thoughts, they were not exaggerated. The Lamanites were a grave threat to the Nephites and had been for many years.

What happened next is remarkable. Alma reassured his people, telling them to stop worrying and stop being afraid. He promised that the Lord would help and deliver them if they would put their trust in Him. The people responded as follows: "Therefore they hushed their fears, and began to cry unto the Lord that he would soften the hearts of the Lamanites, that they would spare them, and their wives, and their children. And it came to pass that the Lord did soften the hearts of the Lamanites" (Mosiah 23:28-29). The people *hushed their fears.* They pleaded with the Lord for deliverance and He eventually provided a way. It's interesting to note that the people were first taken into bondage, forced to bear heavy burdens, and placed under the supervision of harsh taskmasters. It was only after they had been in bondage for a time and endured it well that they were miraculously delivered. But let's go back to the original scene with Alma attempting to comfort his people, analyzing the process step by step.

1. *Something bad happened.* The people were minding their own business and were confronted by an army of their worst enemies.
2. *They listened to words of truth.* As the people went to Alma

for protection and comfort, he taught them true doctrine regarding how God would deliver those who remember Him.

3. *The people acted in faith.* The scripture says, "They hushed their fears" (Mosiah 23:28). It doesn't say "their fears were hushed" or "God made their fears go away." It says *they* did something intentional. They exercised their agency, believing the words of Alma, and did what they could to manage their feelings of anxiety in the moment.
4. *The Lord responded.* He softened the hearts of their enemies so that the people were not immediately killed. Although Alma's people still had to travel a rough road prior to their deliverance, they *were* eventually delivered according to the promises of God.

This is the same pattern that I have hoped to teach throughout this book. Let's apply it to our individual situations:

1. *Something bad happens.* You have anxiety issues. They can be overwhelming. You feel like you cannot control them. There are times when you feel hopeless and helpless.
2. *You listen to words of truth.* The scriptures teach you how to have greater faith. The Lord assures that if we trust Him He will deliver us. Ancient and modern prophets provide messages of hope and peace. You have read such doctrine throughout your life, and much of it is also summarized and explained in what you've read in this book.
3. *You act in faith.* This part is absolutely critical. This is where you recognize your role in managing anxiety. You stop believing that you cannot change. You stop believing that your efforts will not yield results. You *start* doing what you can, even taking very small steps, to move forward and break the patterns of the past. This involves intentional and difficult action on your part. No one can or will do it for you; you must do this part yourself.
4. *The Lord responds.* As you do those things the Lord has asked you to do, His Spirit will bless and change you. You will develop greater capacities. What seemed difficult in the past will start to feel more manageable. You will recognize the hand

of the Lord in your life and forge a stronger partnership with Him. With the two of you linked together in consistent effort, there is nothing you cannot accomplish.

Hope comes from feeling like we can change and move forward. Hopelessness comes from feeling like no matter what we do, nothing is going to improve. I once read something about how baby elephants are trained to become submissive. One of their legs is tied to a pole with a strong rope. The baby elephant tries to escape every which way, but the rope is too strong. Eventually the creature learns it cannot move past the area defined by the rope and resigns itself to staying in that radius. As the elephant grows older, he develops sufficient strength to easily break the rope or even pull the pole clear from the ground. Yet because he has already learned that he cannot escape, *he doesn't try*. The elephant learns to live in captivity, not realizing he has the strength to leave at any time.

I feel this happens to us on occasion. We have been through many experiences that teach us different things about ourselves and our abilities. Some of the things we learn are true and some are inaccurate. For some of you, you have unsuccessfully tried to manage anxiety for many years. You have pulled and pulled against that rope, only finding that you cannot break it. You've accepted this as your lot in life, believing that anxiety is your destiny and you will never get past the small radius defined by the rope. Perhaps many of you have stopped pulling on the rope. You figure you can't break it anyway, so why try? Maybe years or decades have passed since you have made a significant effort to escape.

I don't want anyone to feel this way. I want you to feel there is always hope. There is no rope that cannot be broken as we combine our efforts with the power of the Atonement of Jesus Christ. The scriptures teach, "*For the power is in them*, wherein they are agents unto themselves" (D&C 58:28, emphasis added). *The power is in you.* You have the ability and the obligation to act in your best interest. You are here to change your very nature. You are to shed the natural man and woman and become men and women of Christ. Not only is this our goal and life's mission, it is God's primary purpose as well (see Moses 1:39).

Elder Dieter F. Uchtdorf counseled as follows:

> There may be some among you who feel darkness encroaching upon you. You may feel burdened by worry, fear, or doubt. To you and to all of us, I repeat a wonderful and certain truth: God's light is real. It is available to all! It gives life to all things. It has the power to soften the sting of the deepest wound. It can be a healing balm for the loneliness and sickness of our souls. In the furrows of despair, it can plant the seeds of a brighter hope. It can enlighten the deepest valleys of sorrow. It can illuminate the path before us and lead us through the darkest night into the promise of a new dawn. [16]

He continued: "*Nevertheless, spiritual light rarely comes to those who merely sit in darkness waiting for someone to flip a switch* [emphasis added]. It takes an act of faith to open our eyes to the Light of Christ." [17] Elder Uchtdorf's insights inspire us to hope and also emphasize our accountability. He states the truth that God's light can penetrate any darkness we may experience. It has no bounds and cannot be restrained except through our own unwillingness to accept it. Then he also states that we must act in order to receive that light. We have to throw the switch. Remember, "*Ask*, and ye shall receive" (D&C 4:7, emphasis added). *We* have to ask first. *We* have to act first.

One final scriptural example is instructive in teaching about the importance of our effort, the critical nature of the Lord's timing, and the raw power of His deliverance as it relates to overcoming our challenges, anxiety included. Joseph Smith had a significant question; he wanted to know which of all existing churches was the true church of God. He determined the only way he could truly discover the answer to this question was to ask God directly, through prayer. He had never offered a vocal prayer before. As he knelt down to speak to his Heavenly Father, he was literally attacked by a Satanic force. The force was strong enough to stop him from speaking and enshroud him in darkness. Joseph was overwhelmed by this power, to the point where he felt that he might actually be destroyed. In his own words, he stated, "But, *exerting all my powers* to

16 Dieter F. Uchtdorf, "The Hope of God's Light," *Ensign*, May 2013, 75.

17 Ibid.

call upon God to deliver me out of the power of this enemy which had seized upon me, and *at the very moment* when I was ready to sink into despair and abandon myself to destruction...just at this moment of great alarm, I saw a pillar of light exactly over my head, above the brightness of the sun, which descended gradually until it fell upon me" (JSH 1:16, emphasis added).

Please note two very important phrases in this marvelous account. "Exerting all my powers": Joseph indicates he used every last bit of his physical and emotional strength to resist the evil influence and reach out to God. We don't know how long this struggle lasted. From the description of Joseph's account, it sounds like he had fought long and hard, having given his all. It seems he had nothing left to give and his enemy was going to win. "At the very moment" when Joseph was going to surrender, having struggled as much and as long as he could, he saw a pillar of light. The help didn't come until Joseph was about to give up after having worked as hard as he could.

Along with the pillar of light came something significant. Again, in Joseph's own words, "[The light] no sooner appeared than I found myself delivered from the enemy which held me bound" (JSH 1:17). The light which accompanied the appearance of God the Father and Jesus Christ *immediately* dispelled the powers of darkness. Joseph's mortal efforts to fight the darkness were insufficient, despite the fact he tried his hardest. Yet Satan's powers were not even remotely potent against the formidable presence of God. With Joseph safe and his prior threat contained, the glorious First Vision commenced.

As we review Joseph's experience, we find valuable lessons that apply to our own trials and difficulties. Some of you reading this book have significant anxiety issues. This may be the first or the hundredth book you've read on anxiety management. For those of you who have never made significant efforts to control your anxiety symptoms, you will soon find out just how difficult this can be. For those of you who have tried over and over to change your experience, you may be frustrated at your lack of progress. Perhaps you too feel as if you are being "attacked" or held captive by anxiety symptoms, similar to Joseph's First Vision experience. Remember what happened in his account.

First, he exerted all his powers. To me, that means he fought with everything he had in the moment. In order to successfully manage anxiety, you'll need to do the same. I'm not suggesting you drop everything and devote all your powers to an emotional battle. There are many good things happening in our lives that require time and energy, and we have limited quantities of both. However, you must devote significant time, energy and effort to this cause. Big problems require big solutions. Big solutions need big effort. Don't be deceived that you can change a decades-long pattern of behavior with a couple weeks of casual work. You will have to work hard, work long, and work consistently to eventually develop patterns that will help you effectively manage anxiety.

Second, the Lord intervened but not until it seemed like it was almost too late. The Lord's timing is perfect. I am absolutely convinced that almost *everything* in our lives is carefully choreographed by God the Father, so we can learn and grow most successfully. The timing of Joseph's deliverance was not random. God had watched the whole scene unfold, saw Joseph's struggle, knew that Joseph had tried his hardest and was about to give up, and *then* intervened. What does this mean for you? It means two things. It means that God *will* intervene in your situation. He will provide help and assistance. It also means that such assistance will come with His timing. It may not come until after you have tried and tried with no success. It may not come immediately after you ask for it. *But the help will come.* I am completely confident of this truth. Your Father in Heaven loves you and will help you. He will do it with the most perfect timing possible.

Third, the Lord had power to completely remove Joseph's trial. Satan's most aggressive efforts are no match for God's tremendous glory and majesty. The darkness *always* flees when the light is present. Your trials and your flaws, including anxiety issues, are powerless when heavenly help arrives. Yet that help comes in the Lord's due time. I don't mean to suggest you'll have some remarkable experience like Joseph where you work your hardest, be on the verge of collapse, and then God comes to remove all your anxiety issues. I don't think that is even remotely likely. I *do* think that you will work very hard, come across many times when you feel you can't go any further, and then God will intervene to sustain you for another day. I *do* think that you will work for many weeks, months and even years in your fight against anxiety, learn essential and extremely valuable lessons along the way, and eventually conquer your fears. Through heavenly help, anxiety issues will one day become a thing of the past, either in this life or in the next. Truly your weakness can become your strength (see Ether 12:27).

The timing of the Lord's intervention is up to Him. There is no question regarding His power to completely eradicate anxiety from your life and make you more like Him. The only thing that is left is your effort to engage in the fight. For some of you, the principles and exercises in this book may be sufficient for you to make good progress towards less fear and greater faith. For others, professional help will be essential in that process. Please don't be too afraid or too proud to reach out for professional intervention when needed. As you prayerfully seek His help, your Father in Heaven will direct you towards resources and individuals who can help you learn how to manage anxiety issues and teach you to have a greater quality of life.

My desire is that this book will leave you feeling hopeful. I hope it will give you confidence to move forward. I hope you will look inside yourself and say, "I can do something about my situation. I can act intentionally. As I combine my efforts with the Savior's power, there is nothing we cannot accomplish together." I promise there is always hope. The reality of the Atonement of Jesus Christ means there is always hope. Difficulties may arise in the short and long term. So many of them are designed for your growth, and all of them can be devoted to your eventual learning and progress. Remember the counsel of Lehi to Jacob, "Thou knowest the greatness of God; and he shall consecrate thine afflictions for thy gain" (2 Nephi 2:2).

God bless you as you strive to become more like Him. I promise that His help is available to all who seek Him in faith. I know there is nothing He cannot fix, no ailment He cannot cure and no issue He cannot resolve. You are His child and His first priority. Do your part. Work consistently and intelligently. Be humble and seek revelation. Help is on the way. As Joseph Smith wisely said, "Let us cheerfully do all things that lie in our power; and then may we stand still, with the utmost assurance, to see the salvation of God, and for his arm to be revealed" (D&C 123:17). It is my deepest hope that the Lord's arm and strength be revealed in your life. I promise that it will.

About The Author

David T. Morgan is a licensed psychologist with more than twenty years of experience in the mental health field. He has a BS in psychology, an MS in counseling and guidance, and a PhD in counseling psychology from Brigham Young University. He and his amazing wife are the parents of six children. David loves the scriptures and truly believes the answers to life's challenges can be found in the words of ancient and modern prophets. He also loves Disneyland and knows almost more about the Happiest Place on Earth than he does about psychology.

www.ldspsychologist.com

Made in the USA
Las Vegas, NV
13 February 2022